MAX HEATON

Manifest Lies

*The Unsolved Murder of the
British Journalist David Holden*

www.hugejam.com

Copyright © 2024 by author covered by a legal agreement under English & Welsh law.

Published in England by Huge Jam, 2024
All rights reserved: including, but not limited to, TV, film, drama or media rights in all forms.

No part of this publication may be reproduced, distributed, or transmitted, in any form or by any means, including photocopying, recording, or other electronic or mechanical methods, without the prior written permission of the author, except in the case of brief quotations embodied in critical reviews and certain other non-commercial uses permitted by copyright law. Should there be any infringement of any copyrights committed by this novel then the author confirms that this is unintentional and will address them properly in accordance with English and Welsh law. Regarding any such infringements and for permission requests, please contact the author at holden.manifestlies@gmail.com.

ISBN: 978-1-916604-19-3

This is a fictional novel inspired by, and loosely based on, the real events surrounding the murder of the *Sunday Times* journalist David Holden on 7th December 1977 in Cairo, Egypt. The aim of the novel is to revive interest in this murder and a hope that, after 45 years, it will lead to a proper closure. Most of the characters are real people but a few have had their names altered and some events have been fictionalised. Many details and dates are also altered for literary purposes. Those seeking historical accuracy should not use this novel as a reference. All dialogue is imagined. The author affirms that he has no intention whatsoever to offend or harm anyone, country, belief or creed, mentioned in this novel.

Max Heaton, Author
May 1st 2024

DEDICATION

To David S. Holden,
in the faint hope,
after all the winters,
and the water that's fared under
the forlorn Allenby Bridge,
someone, somewhere, still alive
may have the moral courage,
to tell it all bare.

It is ordained in the eternal constitution of things,
that men of intemperate minds cannot be free.
Their passions forge their fetters.

———————————

Edmund Burke

PART 1

1

Colonel Youssef woke up earlier than usual on the morning of Saturday, 10th December 1977. He had no choice, since his newborn baby son woke everyone up anyway. He'd barely managed a couple of hours sleep. Apart from the opportunity for closeness with his wife Saira that 'going to bed' afforded him, it had been rather pointless, since he had to pick his father up from the airport soon. The newly titled Hajj Hassan was returning from his first Hajj in Mecca and that evening there was to be a big family gathering where respects would be paid accordingly. *It'll be a treat to have some tradition*, thought Youssef. It was otherwise a strange and unsettling Eid holiday – he'd no sooner got used to being a married man in the early spring than he was getting used to being a new father to a winter baby. His wife's strength, beauty and good humour was constantly revealed to him with each new event and emotion, creating a daily sense of excitement within unknown territory.

President Anwar Sadat had seen fit to visit Tel Aviv, the capital city of their 'enemy', on the holiest day of the Muslim calendar: the Day of Arafah. Egyptians now had to believe, apparently, that their life-long antagonist was not the enemy after all. In danger of being overwhelmed, a family gathering was just what Youssef needed to remember who he was and what it was all about. That he had been an officer in the Egyptian CID for three years, ever since national redeployment after the Ramadan – or Yom Kippur – War in October 1973, and that he had been promoted by the then chief of the Security Police.

The phone rang as his young wife was feeding their crying baby, who was clearly demanding more urgency in his mother's attention to her feeding duties. Despite her lack of sleep, Youssef was again struck by her aura. *How can someone glow with weariness?* Saira managed to! She, for her part, had hoped to let her husband get some sleep but the baby Nakeyah rendered that generous, selfless hope fatuous! Instead, Youssef made his way across the lounge from the bedroom, half asleep, murmuring, and answered the phone.

"A'llou?" he almost shouted, his voice not yet adjusting to the breaking day.

"I am sorry to have woken you up, Colonel, but we have *a situation*." It was the Interior Minister and ex-chief of Security Police Nabbawi speaking on the other end of the line.

"Situation, Your Excellency?"

"It's about the man the Cairo department found lying in Darb Al-Ahmar near the new main road, colonel."

"Your Excellency, you rang me about that? I thought it was being taken care of. Major Faisal and his team?"

"Yes, it was. Is. But I personally want you there with him. I don't know much about this Faisal… Hasn't exactly made a name for himself yet. The dead man appears to be an English journalist, rather sensitive just before a peace conference. Murder's not a good look, and there might even be casual talk of espionage."

"Oh, I see, Your Excellency," Youssef yawned those five words unconvincingly, looking at his wife longingly. "Even English journalists can be drunk tourists…"

"Would I, the interior minister, be involving myself at this busy time, and choosing the man for the job, if Cairo – or even Sadat himself – thought that was the case?"

"Sorry, Your Excellency." Faisal flushed and decided to look away from the domestic scene that was calling out to him with its calm warmth. He shook himself into colonel mode. "Please tell me when you need me to be there by." But as he glanced up again and his wife's anxious expression pulled on his heartstrings, he added, "Would tomorrow do, Your Excellency? We have a party for my father tonight. I'm headed to the airport to pick him up now."

Nabbawi replaced the receiver. His face, always austere, showed unusual signs of vulnerability. With his doubts about the unknown Faisal, he hoped that Youssef wasn't about to let him down.

*

It was cold and crisp in Cairo on the morning of December 7th. Three days before Nabbawi's call to Youssef. Each December, an almost cloudless blue sky in Cairo saw many westerners choosing to spend their Christmas break visiting the pyramids, especially now that President Sadat had declared his policy of *infitah*, or "openness to the west". So Major Ahmed Mukhtar Faisal was familiar with dealing with the tendency that rowdy misbehaving European and American tourists had of often ending up in a drunken stupor in the street, forgetting the name of their hotels, or even the name of the city they'd been hell-bent on drinking dry. The worst ones ended up inside a prison cell for the night. But tourism was important for Egypt, and such nuisance was part of the trade-off. It did not occur to Faisal that he would be facing any other problem that day.

It took him forty minutes to get to the scene that had been vaguely described by his sergeant's urgent phone call, hardly half a kilometre behind his office at the police department in Old Cairo. Darb Al-Ahmar was on the border of his jurisdiction but since one of his officers arrived first on the scene, their precinct would undoubtedly get the case. All precincts had recently been put on alert following Sadat's announced peace initiative with Israel. Israeli negotiators being expected in Cairo any day for the Mene House Peace Conference. As a department they were prepared for everything, especially for any trouble by the nationalists, the leftists or the Islamists. The Cairo riots from a few months before were still fresh in the collective memory. The tension was palpable.

The dead man was lying on an unpaved sidewalk along a newly built main road, just behind the fence that marked out the new campus of the ancient Al-Azhar University. The small area was full of soft dune-sand, discarded newspapers and rubbish. But Faisal noticed something he had not seen for some time. Of course, he had seen many dead people in the line of duty, too many in fact, but this one marked itself out. The man looked smart, in a clean corduroy suit and a polo-necked sweater. He was lying on his back almost precisely parallel to the road with his two legs placed close together, arms across his chest, as though he was sleeping. The only disruption in his appearance involved his black-rimmed glasses, which were resting too awkwardly; diagonally over his eyes, as if put on in a hurry. There was a smile on the face of the man, or a smirk rather; it was etched on his frozen face like a sinister touch.

Faisal felt a little uncomfortable. He pushed tentatively against the man with his truncheon, half-expecting him to jump up, but the resistance he felt was that of cold death. His fingers felt no pulse beneath the neat polo neck. He asked everyone to back off and switched up a gear – eyes scanning for clues. Clue one hit him quickly: the man's shoes were clean. That's not to say that the soles were clean, but the uppers were polished and showed no trace of the sandy, dusty powder which was everywhere around. In fact, even his face, his clothes and his hair were missing the fine sand that surrounded him.

"What does that mean, Major?" asked his sergeant.

"It means, Sergeant, that he didn't walk here. Someone must have carried him and placed him here."

"True, good thinking, Major" came his junior's patronising but well-intentioned reply. "How old do you think he is… fifty?"

"Yes, I would say about that, early fifties. We'll know soon, I'm sure. Someone must be missing him by now, a wife, a friend, a tour group. We'll know soon," said Faisal.

In the meantime, Faisal had to wait for the medical officer, Dr. Mohamed Rashid. It was getting warmer now and the doctor took at least an hour to get to the scene through all the traffic. It took him less than a minute to pronounce the man "dead" and label him a *khawajah*, a foreigner.

"Do you have a name for him? Looks very much like a Jim to me!" Perhaps a reference to Carter, the newly sworn-in US president.

"Not yet, we needed your confirmation of death first," Faisal's response sounded strangely embittered. He hated relying on others. Dr. Rashid then scribbled a few notes and left, asking for the dead man to be transferred to the Medical Jurisprudence Department at the notorious Qasr El-Eyni Hospital in Central Cairo.

"I thought that wretched place was closing down?" Faisal remarked.

"Postponed. It's had a three-year reprieve… Needs must and all that…" answered Dr. Rashid just before he departed the crime scene.

Faisal and his sergeant now spoke more freely.

"Do you think he could be American, Major?"

"I don't know, he looks too smug to me, and his clothes are too formal too. An Englishman more likely I'd wager," said Faisal.

"Maybe he'd just attended a formal function, last night, died somehow and some fellow guests left him here, to distance him from the venue… or the host." The sergeant said this as though he'd cracked the case already.

"Possibly," said Faisal, but without giving his sergeant any real attention. He was engrossed in his own theories, and what he would say to his own superior, Colonel Khalid Hasanein, who was known to be a dull, unambitious jobsworth, supremely lacking in the imagination department, and resentful of colleagues who had been blessed with a full quota of it. Hasanein's only desire was to please his immediate boss, General Mohamed Nabbawi Ismail, the man with the "iron fist", the head of the security police; recently promoted by Sadat to interior minister. Moving to his new post only two months ago, history tells us that he would soon impress with his methods for quelling the January riots. Faisal thought that this murder mystery was maybe the break he was waiting for to prove himself: not to Hasanein, but to Minister Nabbawi. Maybe Nabbawi would remember Faisal's father who served with him in the same army brigade, Yemen, 1963… Faisal's mind drifted for a second until his sergeant called him back in.

"Look, Major, there is a hole in his sweater." Faisal regarded what was clearly a small, scorched hole in the polo-necked jumper. Revealed now at the middle of the chest when the garment material was stretched, it had been previously hidden in the folds of the fabric. Faisal has seen these types of holes before, so he turned the body a little to locate a second hole, smaller, cleaner, above the left shoulder. Classic entry and exit bullet holes.

"I think, Sergeant, our 'Jim' has been shot. Look!" Faisal invited his sergeant to look closer. "This now seems more serious than I thought." Faisal ordered the police photographer to take detailed photos of the body's position, while he himself started to check the content of the pockets using his pen. There was nothing! All his pockets were emptied, nada! No passport, no identity, no cards whatsoever. *Strange,* Faisal thought to himself. He then tried to look for something that may have indicated Jim's nationality but, again, nothing!

"Look at his clothes' labels, maybe you can tell from those…" His sergeant told him there were no labels on his clothes and even the maker of his glasses could not be identified. *An unidentified European man shot dead in Cairo,* thought Faisal. *That's all we need now.* Americans, Israeli negotiators, the UN were all due to arrive in Cairo anytime. *This is not the publicity Cairo needs...* Faisal's initial enthusiasm about the case being his launchpad to higher things waned.

Police photography finished, the body was carefully removed from the scene, put in an ambulance and taken to Qasr El-Eyni. The cordon was removed and the road soon returned to its usual busy self as if nothing had been investigated there on Wednesday, December 7th 1977. The nearby muezzins were soon calling for the noon prayer.

2

The news of "an unidentified European man shot dead in Cairo" soon reached Colonel Hasanein who immediately briefed Minister Nabbawi. The minister was naturally alarmed, the killing of foreigners, especially westerners, was rare in Egypt. Robbery or fights were all too common, but not killing. It was bad publicity, at the worst possible time. Nabbawi knew he had to inform the President when he met him later that day for his weekly briefing about the internal security situation and the activities of the opposition. He knew that in this part of the world, it was more critical for civil servants like to him to avoid blame than to actually make an executive decision. And Sadat enjoyed being told everything!

"Keep an eye on this case, Hasanein, we need to be ahead of this and wrap this up quickly. I'm going to get Colonel Youssef to take over the case" Nabbawi said.

"Your Excellency, no need for Youssef... It is most likely a robbery gone wrong, Your Excellency, there is no doubt in my mind about it... his pockets were fleeced! Expect a quick result from our boys," the low-key Colonel Hasanein answered while Nabbawi, ignoring him, felt he had to spell out the actions to be taken next. Nabbawi had little confidence in Hasanein's comprehension of complex police matters.

"Contact all the big hotels and ask if they have a guest missing, someone who didn't come back last night... oh and see if any of the informants picked up on any chatter about a westerner being mugged." Nabbawi added, "Make sure you update me daily... or immediately if anything new crops up!" Hasanein, ever obedient, saluted his superior most precisely and left.

Faisal for his part was trying to rush things along too, chasing the medical officer at Qasr El-Eyni Hospital and urging him to perform an autopsy. But Qasr El-Eyni was an archaic institution, where only one task a day could be managed, and transferring the body to the morgue was that day's task.

Qasr El-Eyni has seen better days, but not since Napoleon's general, Kleber, was buried here, thought Faisal as he entered the hospital via its front garden. Seeing Jim's naked body lying on the old and stained terrazzo slab of the morgue, with outdated, rusty equipment scattered around it reminded him of a Frankenstein movie he once saw, but Faisal kept that cultural reference to himself.

"I've got so many autopsies piling up Major. Long overdue. I can do it for you the day after tomorrow."

"Nope. No good, Doctor. The minister is on our case and expecting us to brief him daily. Do you fancy telling him the body is cooling in the fridge nicely, undisturbed?" Dr. Rashid finally relented to the pressure and agreed to book the autopsy for first thing on Thursday 8th December.

But Faisal should've known better than to push an Egyptian civil servant into doing something quickly. The retribution would be the worst quality results, a "brush for the rush"; exactly what Faisal dreaded when he arrived early the next morning to witness the autopsy.

"A single gunshot to the heart, that's what killed him, Major. 9mm most likely..." With those words the medical examiner opened and shut his portion of the case and started writing his notes.

"And time of death?" asked Faisal,

"It will all be in my report if you can just be patient," snapped Dr. Rashid as, to Faisal's surprise, he asked his assistant to take the body away.

"What do you mean? Is that it? Aren't you going to open him up?"

"Why would I need to do that? You want us to cause a diplomatic incident? What if his folks find out we opened him up already? What if he is an American? Do you want negative press right now?" But, seeing the look on Faisal's face Rashid added, "If this is what you want then get me a ministerial directive. Only the Minister has the power to overturn my decision."

Faisal didn't respond. A few moments later he accepted the carbon copy Dr. Rashid handed him of his report, in Arabic of course:

> An unidentified western-looking male likely to be in late 40s, or early 50s, shot dead with a single gunshot bullet, aimed at the heart, with a 9mm entry wound from a place around 4cm from the centre of his left armpit at the back and an exit wound at the front chest somewhere between the fourth and fifth ribs missing the sternum by 15mm. There are signs of bruising on the victim's knuckle and fingers, on his left arm, and less on his right consistent with defensive wounds and indicating that the victim may have been left-handed. More details can be established when the bullet is found and the circumstances of his death are better known. Time of death is estimated between 3am to 5am Wednesday morning 7 December 1977. Photographs of the scene and victim to follow this report once the films are developed and printed.
>
> Conclusion: death due to an unlawful act.

Faisal, confused between the acrid stench of blood and everything else in the autopsy theatre and reading the report, barely focused on Dr. Rashid's next words.

"Well, okay, let me know if the Minister wants me to carry out a full autopsy… but it's not really required, not in my opinion anyway." Dr. Rashid half-turned, then added: "Oh, yes, good that I remembered, his clothes and personal belongings are all in a plastic bag ready for you to log them in the evidence room. They were too contaminated with dune sand to get any meaningful results out of them; just some specks of blood, his own I expect, and yes, we did find something in his pockets… some foreign coins in the small pocket of his cords." Then he swept out of the dilapidated autopsy theatre with the urgency and self-consciousness of an actor who had just delivered a knockout line.

Faisal, alone and stunned, was sure he went through Jim's pockets thoroughly. Maybe he missed one. The embarrassment of having to tell his superior, Colonel Hasanein, that they missed something. He took the plastic bag, laid the contents out on a table. Apart from the glasses he could only see clothes. He put on medical gloves and started rummaging through the clothes, now creased. He then checked the labels and could see they had all been forcibly removed, but neatly so, with scissors or a sharp knife. Apart from some English numbers on the inside arm of the glasses, there was no brand name to indicate their manufacturer or origin. He finally spotted the coins, taking them one by one – four pieces of various sizes – noting the profile of a man printed on them with print marks across the top, *The Hashemite Kingdom of Jordan.*

At the station, Faisal wrote his notes accompanied by the background noise of a typical Cairo office and the smell of strong coffee. Not only did he know the time of Jim's death, but also that he was in Jordan at some point before coming to Egypt. And it seemed the killer had emptied his victim's pockets, without checking the smallest of them. *A sign of hurriedness, maybe? But the cutting of the clothes labels using scissors indicates careful pre-planning. Could it have been a premeditated robbery? By someone who knew who to kill and what they were killing for? Money is the most likely motive,* thought Faisal. *But ripping the labels off the clothes? Why? And how many perpetrators?* Faisal couldn't shake from his mind the thought that this had been a robbery committed by a gang. He decided to brief his superior and start investigating in earnest... But first, he should establish Jim's real name.

Minister Nabbawi was his usual irritated self when he called Hasanein and Faisal to his office. "Did any of the hotels get back to you confirming a missing guest? Someone must be missing him... it's been two nights now?"

"We checked and no! Your Excellency, we need more time."

"And *this* is exactly what we *don't* have! Time! Also this is not a good *'time'* to have something like this on our hands. The world's media blaming 'us' for a foreigner's death... The President himself has voiced his concern by the way. Go ahead and inform the Ministry for Foreign Affairs to issue a brief description of the incident to all embassies in Cairo."

"Right away, Your Excellency. Consider it done," said Faisal, saluting and taking his leave even more hastily than usual.

Thus it was that on Friday December 9th, all foreign embassies in Cairo received a telex from the Egyptian Foreign Affairs Ministry:

AN UNIDENTIFIED MALE BELIEVED TO BE EUROPEAN AND APPEARING IN HIS EARLY 50S FOUND DEAD IN CAIRO ON WEDNESDAY 7 DECEMBER. PLEASE CONTACT US IF THIS CONCERNS YOU.

The First Secretary at the British Embassy in Cairo was a young diplomat in his thirties, just promoted. He was alerted to the telex content by the assistant on duty that Friday afternoon. Something rang a bell.

"Hmmm, I had a phone call from the Sunday Times in London last night asking if we knew the whereabouts of their chief foreign correspondent who hadn't reported to his hotel in Cairo on Tuesday night as planned. Better give the Ministry in London a quick call."

The wheels of communication were set in motion and soon gained momentum. It wasn't long before the First Secretary was contacting the Sunday Times directly, to speak with the chief editor there, Harold Evans.

"The man you are looking for in Cairo, what's his name again?"

"David, David Shipley Holden, head of the Middle East news desk. Did you find him?"

"It might be something and nothing but Egyptian authorities have just informed us that they have found an unidentified body, a man." Evans sunk into total silence, shocked. *"Hello? Are you still there?"*

"Sorry, yes, don't know what to say…" mumbled Evans.

"Do you know anyone in Cairo who could identify him? The quicker we get on top of this the better, if you know what I mean."

"Oh… Yes, true… Let me think… I am sure we can arrange that. I'll telex you the details shortly."

Looking out from the window of his London office, a gloomy cloud drew closer over the sky as Evans juggled his thoughts, replacing the telephone receiver, unsure if he should tell Holden's wife, Ruth, who was also working with them as a photojournalist. *But what if the body turns out to be a false alarm?* He thought. *I'd be upsetting her, not to mention David, unnecessarily.* Instead, he managed to find two people in Cairo who knew Holden well: Bob Jobbins, the BBC man in Cairo, and Imad Jawhar of Reuters. Both knew Holden in person and both agreed to the gruesome task. As directed by Evans, they contacted the British Embassy to arrange a visit to the morgue for Saturday morning. Almost instantly they were shown the body, Jobbins and Jawhar confirmed the dreadful news to Evans and Jim had a new name: David Shipley Holden. He was an Englishman, as Faisal had first thought.

3

Faisal had his break now! Or so he thought.

But was this case too big and sensitive for his department and someone of his rank to deal with? This was not about the murder of a hapless tourist anymore, it was about the murder of a well-known British journalist who had probably been there to cover Sadat's peace initiative with Israel. It could even be a political murder. The State Security Investigation Department would surely be involved now and may take the case from him.

Faisal's suspicions were confirmed when his superior, Colonel Hasanein, told him exactly that. Minister Nabbawi had assigned the case to a new investigator, the rising star of the Egyptian CID, Colonel Nabil Hassan Ali Youssef. "It's for the best, Ahmed, we have enough on our plate as it is, there will be nothing but headaches from a case like this, let them handle it and make a mess of it as usual…" Hasanein sniggered the last few words, and he had a point. The State Security Investigation Department in Egypt was notorious for using one method of investigation to get quick results, "torture all witnesses and see who will squeak first". Minister Nabbawi believed in this method too, as did Sadat. Nabbawi called it "humane methods of pressure" to make his prisoners "fear" the wrath of the state, and if need be "feel" it, with emphasis more on the psyche than the physical. Faisal didn't object too much to using this method, it was a quick method, saving time and effort, but Faisal knew it didn't always give the full truth – often just the bare minimum as innocents suffered and admitted to anything in order to get out. Faisal believed in using other methods, more 'humane' and 'scientific'.

Colonel Youssef was a good detective, no doubt, but rumour had it that he belonged to the Nabbawi school of "humane torture", believing, by all accounts, that only a police state could be viable in the Arab world and that it could only exist if it instilled fear of the state, or *haibah*, into the heart of the people. Haibah was a term Youssef had coined for it, in one of the lectures he had given a few months before to the police academy as part of his recent promotion. Fortune had smiled. He fitted Nabbawi's vision for reforming the police force in Egypt at that time.

This rising star was at that moment celebrating his father's return from Mecca. Hajj Hassan arrived home with stories for everyone of his experience and shared many lessons that he'd learned during the pilgrimage. Despite being tired from the long journey, he was ready to enjoy a night of celebration and thanksgiving with his family.

The get-together was filled with laughter and traditional Egyptian food. Youssef enjoyed watching his father interact with everyone, including his new grandson who slept peacefully despite the cacophony of voices. After the meal, Hajj Hassan called Youssef over to the balcony. Looking up at the clear, star-peppered Middle Eastern night sky together, his father recounted the sights and sounds of his Saudi Arabian journey that he'd saved for sharing with just his son and told how he'd come back feeling renewed. Youssef had been moved deeply by this moment of connection with his father and he'd realised how lucky he was to have such a family. He made a vow to himself that no matter how hard life got, he would never forget what his family had done for him and make sure that he provided the same love and commitment to his own family. His recent promotion was a good start. He looked across at Saira, nursing Nakeyah so naturally, and felt his strong attraction to her newfound maternal plumpness. He had always been attracted to women slightly older than himself, and the maturity of motherhood had made his young wife even more desirable to him. Something she felt from him each night, despite their tiredness. Near midnight, Saira announced that it was time for everyone to make du'a together as a family and the long, glorious evening ended.

*

First thing Monday, Faisal had to undergo the agony of having to hand over his precious case and endure Youssef's questions as he did so. This Youssef prodigy was so young that Faisal, a year older, resented even more the feeling that he was being condescended to. He'd been hoping he might get to continue with the case in some role: with the energy he'd shown from the start, he felt he could help solve it or at least help with the groundwork. But Youssef was non-committal on that score, saying simply that he would see if he needed any help from a "uniformed officer". And that was that. Colonel Youssef had become the lead investigator on the case reporting directly to Minister Nabbawi; the latter being asked to brief the President, bright-shining colonel in tow, on the same day.

Monday December 12th was a public holiday, New Year's Day according to the Islamic Hijri calendar. Sadat had promised to give a press conference updating the world with the progress of his peace negotiations with the Israelis who had arrived in Cairo to prepare the ground for the upcoming peace conference. It was in this context that Nabbawi and Youssef arrived at the President's residence late evening to brief him on Holden's murder.

"Heh ya Nabbawi? Arrested anyone?" asked President Sadat of Nabbawi, who was exhibiting his usual exaggerated deference.

"Not yet, Your Excellency, Mr. President, the evidence…"

"Evidence? You're still collecting evidence?" Sadat interrupted. "A man was killed shortly after arriving at Cairo Airport, surely there's a huge amount of evidence, not one piece but a veritable mountain?!"

Youssef stepped in and answered, "Your Excellency, Mr. President, this is the point, there is something unusual about this case… it was as if the man vanished from the airport."

"But he reappeared… as a corpse! And in the middle of Cairo! Surely many people saw something, this is Cairo after all," exclaimed Sadat. Nabbawi stumbled over his words as Youssef, unshaken, addressed Sadat directly.

"Your Excellency, Mr. President, I recommend you postpone your press conference and maybe even the peace conference, until we know more about this murder." Nabbawi stood alongside the upstart astounded, listening, totally frozen with fear of upsetting the President, but surprisingly, Sadat turned his head to Youssef and lowered the tone of his voice,

"Why, my son… this might be received in many different ways if we delay. You do know how much is at stake here?"

"Yes, Your Excellency, Mr. President, that's exactly why I am saying this. Your safety is at stake!"

"How so?" asked Sadat, half intrigued and half put out by Youssef's precociousness.

"Holden was planning to attend the conference today, but we know now he was murdered. How can we be sure that his killers might have stolen his credentials so as to enter the conference and target you, Your Excellency? It is too soon for us to increase security now and if we double-check the identity of each and every journalist there will be some negative fallout. I suggest we postpone and, if the perpetrators did steal his credentials, then they will know that their trick has been exposed. If they didn't, then perhaps a day or two's delay can be explained somehow."

President Sadat paused and turned to the commander of his personal guard who was sitting with them listening and nodding in agreement with this colonel's logical thought processes. The Colonel certainly had the ability to convince him with minimal persuasion. Sadat postponed the conference by two days and his press office issued a short statement:

> The competent authorities in Egypt will not leave a stone unturned until the perpetrators of this heinous crime against a reputable journalist on our soil is found and punished appropriately.

Meanwhile, Nabbawi contacted Merlyn Rees, the British Home Secretary under Prime Minister Callaghan: "I wish to express my deep sorrow for the assassination of Mr. David Holden. Please pass my condolences to his family and his colleagues at the Sunday Times. Rest assured, Mr. Rees, that we have appointed our best investigators to this top-priority case and hope to show you some results in a matter of days. Please tell me if you need anything more from us."

"Thank you, Mr. Nabbawi, for your kind sentiments, I will be sure to pass them on. I have every confidence in your police work; we too have appointed a team of investigators who will be happy to join your team in Cairo, if you will allow it of course."

"I will of course give your kind proposal some consideration and get back to you. Who knows, perhaps my team might need to come to London as part of their investigation too? We certainly need to coordinate ourselves to resolve this mystery, and quickly."

But the truth is, what Colonel Youssef was facing now in dealing with the murder of Holden was totally different from what Major Faisal had faced in investigating 'Jim'. Not only was Youssef under direct pressure from the President to solve this murder-mystery quickly but the media shock-reaction around the world didn't make it easier for him either. Many newspapers, especially in Lebanon, with their raging civil war, were already claiming to have solved the crime. New theories appeared every day! The Sunday Times of course felt a moral obligation to help and decided to form their own journalist investigation teams in many of the Arab capitals. The British Home Secretary even appointed two investigators from Scotland Yard. All of this was too much for Youssef to handle all at once, so Nabbawi provided him with a team of investigators of which, and with Youssef's agreement, Faisal was one.

Yes, Youssef was overwhelmed by the avalanche of information, but he was systematic and methodical in his approach. His sixth sense told him that the key to solving Holden's murder resided in knowing the motive. The prima facie evidence was clearer: a murder of a British journalist in Egypt covering the run up to the Mene House Peace Conference between the Egyptians and Israelis. Accordingly, Youssef divided his team into three units according to his categorisation of the motives: *money, sex,* and *politics.*

Faisal led the money team, exploring the options of just a simple robbery gone wrong. The sex angle was led by Captain Sayyed Hassan Mahmoud, a promising young officer. The investigation into the possibility of a political motive was led by Youssef himself, since it was the likeliest and most sensitive of all. In order to make sure they were all on the same page, Youssef held two daily briefings, one in the morning to plan for the day ahead and another late evening to take stock of the intervening day's findings. Apart from Minister Nabbawi, Youssef kept everyone outside his team totally in the dark and asked his team for total secrecy in their findings, "We are dealing with a sensitive murder, we must treat everything as secret. If in doubt, come and ask me. Officers, remember we must draw a fine line between criminal investigation and journalistic curiosity. The victim is a journalist, a well-known one by the sounds of it, and journalists are just like us, gentlemen… they get agitated when one of their own gets hurt, let alone killed in this way."

4

Youssef and his team only started working in earnest from 13th December – after the Islamic new-year holiday, Muharram – almost a week after the murder. He wanted everyone to be fully conversant with the cold hard facts and less susceptible to wayward emotions or conjecture.

"Major Faisal," Youssef said loudly in front of the whole team. "You dealt with the case from the start, please brief the team on what we know so far." Again, an instinctive sense for how to get people on side – this time with an indiscernible flattery.

Faisal jumped as he stood up, "Sir", and addressed the team: "Officers, a British man named David Shipley Holden, born November 30th 1924 – making him 53 – a famous journalist, head of the Middle East news desk of a prominent newspaper in London called the Sunday Times, a sister of The Times which as we all know is one of the most respectable newspapers in the world…" Faisal caught his breath and then continued: "According to his employers, Holden boarded a plane in Amman, Jordan, on Tuesday evening, December 6th. The flight was a Royal Jordanian Airlines flight number RJ503 from Amman to Cairo. It left at 20:40 hours local time, arriving in Cairo at 23:12 hours local time. Holden applied for a normal visitor's visa, entered the country, exchanged $200 in Barclays Bank travellers' cheques for Egyptian currency – this all being around a few minutes before midnight. This was his last known sighting. Presumably he left the airport, must have got into a car, a taxi most likely, but no one witnessed any of that." Faisal then finished confidently, filling them in on how they had found Holden, how they had identified him, and anything else he knew.

"What was the purpose of his visit?" came one officer's question.

"The Sunday Times says he was here to cover the peace conference…"

"Why such a late flight?" shouted another a voice.

"No particular reason… There was a delay at Amman airport for some reason or another, but it had nothing to do with the plane itself or the case, if this is what your question implies Officer," answered Faisal.

"How did a journalist slip through our airport security?" asked Mahmoud.

"Very good question, Captain," answered Faisal. "Our Ministry of Information had in fact set up a special section in arrivals to receive journalists coming to cover the peace conference. But it seems our victim chose to write on his visa application that his profession was "writer" not "journalist" as he should have. That's how he slipped through the net. He'd probably be alive right now if he'd just stated the truth." Faisal's voice was now competing with the noise of a team adding its own comments.

"Did he do this deliberately though? I'm sure the Ministry of Information would have had a list of journalists for passport control prepared in advance, so they'd know who the visitors were regardless of what they'd written under 'profession'?"

"More good questions, Captain," said Faisal, much to the chagrin of the rest of the team. "So let me answer them one at a time. We don't know Holden's motivation for putting down "writer" as his profession, but his Sunday Times colleagues claim he was on a sabbatical to write a book about Saudi Arabia, and he had travelled already to a few places in the world for that purpose, so it wasn't a complete lie. But he lied about the purpose of his visit to Cairo this time, that's for sure, since strictly speaking he didn't come here to write. Now, was it deliberate? Well, the reception committee for members of the press at the airport is not well organised if you ask me. Many try to avoid it due to the time they take to process names, so we can assume that he may have done this deliberately to avoid them. There could be another reason of course, but one thing is for sure, this half-truth cost him his life."

"And the second half of my question?" pressed Captain Mahmoud.

"Yes, there was a list prepared by the Ministry of Information and they issued it to our colleagues at airport security, but that list kept changing and more names were crossed out and replaced with others until, and I am assuming here, our colleagues at airport security had given up checking them. They relied on their security records only and Egypt had no problem with Mr. David Holden entering the country…" Faisal was convincing; the team went quiet.

"So we know nothing of the victim's movements? From the moment he left the airport, up to the point where he was found dead near the Al-Azhar campus?" asked another officer.

"Has anyone talked to the taxi drivers, the registered ones, to see if they know which taxi was taken by the victim and where it took him?" asked a different officer.

"That's a problem, Officer. Not a single registered taxi driver from the airport has claimed to be aware of the victim's arrival let alone where he went; we can only assume he didn't take a registered taxi… or if he did, it was possibly one of those 'gypsy' taxis that cruise around, you know, dropping one fare off and picking up another at the same time, which of course suggests an unplanned murder."

"What about his hotel booking?" asked a voice from the back of the room.

"We understand from his colleagues, that he had two hotel bookings and lost them both due to continually changing his itinerary when he was in Jordan, one with the Hilton and the other with the Meridien," Faisal said. "So although we need to double-check both, it seems that he arrived in Cairo thinking that his final booking was with the Meridien Hotel. He left London Heathrow on Sunday November 27th for Damascus… then went to Jordan by car, with a short detour to the West Bank, before going back to Jordan and then arriving here. But officers, all this needs to be checked and corroborated."

Youssef then addressed his team: "You can see how there's a lot at stake," he told them, "and many countries are waiting for our results. But above all, our president is expecting us to wrap this up as soon as possible."

Faisal ended his part of the briefing with an overview of the robbery as a motive: the victim's pockets had been emptied, he'd had $200 worth of Egyptian currency, and a large amount of travellers' cheques on him. Despite the amount of money involved, the cheques were traceable so useless for thieves. Faisal then concluded: "We must also cover the basic angle of who might benefit from the victim's death, it could be someone related to the victim himself like his wife or a brother." Youssef thanked Faisal for his clear account of the status quo and asked for a list of questions to be prepared and sent to London.

Captain Mahmoud's turn with a précis of the sexual angle took less than a minute. Holden, by colleagues' accounts, was a married man, a serious man, and no one was aware of extramarital affairs. This left Youssef to wrap up the briefing by intimating that a political motive was the most likely and could be approached in a variety of ways; not least regarding the victim's intention to cover the peace conference. But there was the politics of the man himself. Holden, a reputable journalist, was known to Egypt already. True he had been critical of President Nasser with some sharp and witty articles – actually he was detained briefly during the Suez Crisis in 1956, according to Egyptian records – but Holden was generally friendlier to the Egypt of Sadat, and he had not said anything that would warrant state revenge.

As a Western journalist, it was natural that he'd know many people from different backgrounds: Russians, Americans, Israelis, Egyptians, Syrians, Iraqis, Palestinians and many more. But it was Holden's relationship with the Palestinians that drew Youssef's attention. He was known to have sympathies with the Palestinian cause, "he felt they had a raw deal" one of his colleagues told them later. He believed firmly that the Palestinians were the victims of the settlements that had followed the two World Wars in Europe, holding Arab leaders equally complicit in the plan devised by Henry Kissinger that liquidated the Palestinian cause and turned it from a political issue to a humanitarian problem. When, later that day, Youssef met with Holden's colleagues, Cal McCrystal and John Bailey, the victim's politics loomed larger.

The two Sunday Times journalists had come to Cairo to help the investigation and undertake their own on behalf of the Sunday Times, determined to find out what happened to their colleague. They confirmed that his later articles had been one on South Yemen and another, written jointly with others, on the torture of 49 Palestinian prisoners in Israel. They went on to share with Youssef what they knew about Holden's meetings in Amman and his last-minute change of plan to visit the West Bank. Youssef started to bet with himself that there were two potential suspects wanting to liquidate Holden: the Palestinian Rejectionists who have rejected Sadat's peace initiative with Israel, or the Israeli Mossad themselves due to the victim's sympathies with the Palestinians. He was anxious to discover what the Palestinians in the West Bank thought about Sadat's peace initiative. But he knew all these details would faze most of his men, so he quickly turned back to less abstract details.

Later in the day, in the second investigation team briefing, Youssef addressed his colleagues. "Officers, we are most likely looking for a gang. It's impossible for a person to have committed this crime alone…

it also has signs of careful planning. So we must start at two points: where Holden was last known to be alive, the exact spot at the airport, and move forward, and also where he was found dead too, behind Al-Azhar University, and move backward. We must interview all taxi drivers, all airport security people and employees, as well as those at the location where the body was found. It's a busy road after all, someone must have seen something. Copies of the victim's photograph are now printed for you to take with you, please show these to as many people as you can, and we'll regroup later today."

Youssef first assumed that Holden must have left the airport voluntarily since no one noticed anything untoward there. He most likely did what most arriving passengers do and took a taxi to the Meridien hotel; a proper registered taxi… it is unlikely for a Western visitor to jump in a 'gypsy' taxi at such a late time of night. Even most Egyptians would think twice about doing that! Youssef's political unit detained and questioned all the registered taxi drivers who had taken fares to the Meridien that night – easy since all their journeys were recorded by the police – but they found nothing unusual and the hotel confirmed to them that all bookings had checked in. Then doubts started to set in.

"What if we got this wrong, Colonel?" Faisal confided in Youssef. "What if Holden himself had got mixed up, and thought his booking was with the Hilton, and not the Meridien as his colleagues told us?" This was exactly the sort of question Youssef was looking for. He smiled his approval and Faisal felt the validation from the young man as a warm glow. Why was it so impossible to resent this colonel? With that suggested change of tack they sure enough found one taxi driver who had picked up three foreign tourists from the airport for the Hilton… but only two had checked in. Still, further interrogation was unproductive, as it turned out the third person had checked into a different hotel and, in the end, everyone was accounted for. Another dead end. More doubts.

Youssef deliberately didn't share with his political unit during either briefing his meeting with the President, despite Sadat's words still ringing in his ears. They didn't need that kind of pressure yet. *The President has a point,* he kept thinking to himself though. *How can a man just vanish in Cairo without anyone noticing?*

5

Now Youssef felt tremendous pressure, from all sides. The night before the peace talks were to start at Mene House, at their revised date, he received a phone call from Minister Nabbawi. "The President wants an update, let us go together and meet him."

"Sure, Your Excellency, when?"

"Now!" said Nabbawi as if surprised by the question. "I shall meet you there… Wait, also, let *me* do the talking this time."

Youssef prepared himself for a dressing down from the president for not having nailed Holden's killers, but presidential rails and rants were water off a duck's back to this colonel. He was more than used to the blindness that often blights those government bosses who just want results at any cost, just so long as the cost wasn't a weakening of their own position. Youssef was tough too and wasn't going to be emasculated by a scared and fretting president.

Inside his office suite, Sadat was clearly busy with myriad briefings about the upcoming conference, attending to details as small as making sure the Israeli guests would be offered kosher food. Youssef was surprised that such details were being dealt with by the president, until it became clear that even meat was political: "Make sure they are well fed, we don't want them complaining. Also people tend to give more concessions when their stomachs are full." As his chief of staff, Hassan Kamal, was leaving for the kitchens, the smiling president added, "And make sure the synagogue is clean when they visit it!"

As Sadat turned to the two men in front of him his smile faded, as expected. Less expected was the absence of staff to witness the conversation. In fact, it seemed Sadat was anxious that no one should overhear, and he kept looking over his shoulder. "What is this, ya Nabbawi? This investigation into Holden's killing is taking too long, I am getting embarrassed, I gave the whole world my word that I'd catch the killer quickly."

"Killers, Your Excellency Mr. President, not one, but several."

"All the more reason to have caught them by now... surely someone would have squeaked... with your techniques, ya Nabbawi."

Youssef interjected. "Your Excellency Mr. President, if I may, our initial findings so far indicate that this murder is an international crime, not an Egyptian one, the killers could be anywhere in the world by now." Nabbawi froze, in the manner of a parent whose toddler had come out with an expletive.

Sadat seized the unintended bait. "What? Do you mean that this murder was carried out without a single Egyptian involved, Youssef?"

"No Your Excellency Mr. President. While we may catch the Egyptian actors involved, and probably soon, we might never put our hands on the masterminds, the men in the international shadows, unless we widen the investigation to cross borders."

Sadat was distracted by a thought. "That reminds me, Prime Minister Callaghan has contacted me. The UK is complaining about a perceived lack of progress, and poor communication. Scotland Yard formed an investigation team in London and are asking us to grant them permission to come and work with you gentlemen in Cairo, with Sunday Times journalists too. We need to keep them sweet and calm them down. Nabbawi, I want you to grant them permission! They also want us to send Holden's body back to his wife..."

"With great respect Your Excellency Mr. President, I advise against this," said Youssef emphatically, to Nabbawi's growing annoyance. Sadat sensed Nabbawi's annoyance and waved to him to be remain quiet; the President was more impressed with Youssef every time he met him. *I need people like him,* he thought. *Youssef is confident, independent and a free thinker; he makes a change from the mentally lethargic officers who plague the state, a Nasser legacy.* Sadat motioned to Youssef to continue,

"David Holden was British, yes, but he was likely killed for reasons which have nothing to do with Egypt, or possibly not even the peace conference. The best we can hope for is that this case was a 'robbery gone wrong'... but the crime has the modus operandi of a foreign intelligence agency too, and we have to rule this in, for now. Granted it could most likely be the Palestinian extremists, but the British Intelligence aren't out of the mix. Do you, Your Excellency Mr. President, want us to grant access to players who are potentially the killers themselves? Allowing them to manipulate our investigation? As for the Sunday Times crowd, I met some of them, I wouldn't trust them as far as I can throw them! They could be just as implicated."

Sadat, Faisal, and even Nabbawi were stunned by the clarity and reasoning behind Youssef's thinking. They paused, themselves thinking about the profoundness of what had just been said.

Sadat broke the silence. "What to do then? I promised them."

"And you will keep that promise, Your Excellency Mr. President... we will just stall them and hide behind their perception of our 'Arab incompetence', let them revel in their prejudice against us, it is better that, than have them meddling with our investigation." As if remembering rank, Sadat turned back to Nabbawi.

"Mohamed, make sure we sweet talk the British. I leave it to you to talk to Merlyn Rees. Release the body back to London at least and in the meantime tell Rees that instead of their working party coming to Cairo we will go to them. Let Youssef go to London as a smoke screen, to show them we are doing something. Brief me in two days' time." There was a tell-tale spring in Nabbawi's step as he left the presidential grounds. Could it be that he too was impressed by Youssef, his rising star?

*

The next day, Thursday December 15th, saw a shift in gear. Youssef finally got the breakthrough he desperately needed. This coincided with media attention shifting from the "old news" of Holden's murder to the Mene House Peace Conference that was now on its first full day. It promised to be newsworthy. The Mene House Oberoi Hotel with its palm trees and Moorish architecture was ten miles out of central Cairo and, rather unfortunately for Egypt's tourists, at the foot of the Giza pyramids. As if the worst December weather in memory, with leaden grey skies and slanting rain, wasn't enough, in addition to the 1000-strong security presence around the venue, the main road to the pyramids was closed for the duration.

The political fallout was of the kind to interest the population at large and sell papers: five empty seats at the table with Jordan, Syria, Lebanon, the PLO, and the USSR refusing to attend; the Israelis refusing to recognise the PLO flag; a flurry of confusion as organisers wondered if they'd confused the Jordanian flag with the Yemeni one, and place names at the table being abandoned last-minute because it wasn't considered wise to label anything with the word Palestine.

Faisal had received a phone call from the Al-Duqqi police department, an affluent area in Cairo. A resident there had reported an abandoned car. The police had established that the car was stolen and were holding the original owner. Faisal asked them angrily why on earth they thought the car could be connected to Holden's case.

"Sir," came the reply. "The car itself was stolen, but when we contacted the owner to take it back, he told us that instead of its contents having been stolen as he feared, the car came back to him with even more stuff inside it! Stuff that seems to belong to a foreigner. You better come and see for yourself, sir."

A Fiat Nasr 128, recently painted white, greeted Faisal and Youssef as they arrived in Al-Duqqi. Registration number Gizah District 336171. This type of car was the most common in Egypt, mass-assembled in Egyptian factories and ubiquitous in the street scenes of Cairo. This one was a 1972 model, relatively new, so it was strange to find it repainted unless it had "been in an accident", or "used for murder recently". At least, so thought Youssef and Faisal as they asked everyone to *step away from the car*. This caused a degree of amusement among Al-Duqqi officers since the 'world and his wife' had touched it, even sat inside it, ever since they'd found it. The triangular quarter light window of the front passenger side was broken and a bundle of wires could be seen hanging below the dashboard.

The owner of the car was Nagib Mustafa Ahmad, a twenty-two-year-old second-year engineering student at Cairo University. He was standing a distance away with a police officer as though under arrest. He had a Jordanian passport, but was Palestinian in origin, from Safad. Although the car was legally in his name, he appeared to share the car with his fiancée, Wifaq Abdulla Meshal, and her brother, Farooq. They too were Palestinians with Jordanian passports, and they all lived together in one apartment. As the implications of his car having been used in the murder he'd been reading about in the newspapers became clearer, Nagib became more scared. As if in dramatic sympathy with the young Palestinian couple, the weather was forecast to deteriorate. A rainstorm was threatening. Youssef ordered that the car and its owners be transferred to the Cairo station immediately.

On their way back, Faisal said to Youssef: "It's just as I thought then. It's the Palestinian extremists who did it, they killed Holden, it must be, it's clear to me now!" Youssef kept quiet, thinking, while Faisal ran on as if the case was now closed for good. Youssef had learnt from experience that the worst thing any investigator can do is to close a case too early without a thorough assessment. Things were certainly moving in the direction of Faisal's theory though. Nagib's maternal uncle turned out to be Salah Khalaf, Palestine's answer to Trotsky, a left-wing senior member of Fattah who had been expelled from Egypt a few years before due to his political activities. That wasn't all. This is what Youssef wrote in his notebook as to what they found in the boot of the stolen car, along with a discarded front seat headrest that didn't belong to the car (it had a different fabric). There was no sign of any blood. "A large red-colour Samsonite suitcase, the type that opens in two equal halves, with jumbled clothes inside, two wrapped Christmas gifts, an Olivetti portable typewriter, some unexposed rolls of film, a blue folder with a letter inside and some notes, in English, mainly about Saudi Arabia, and finally many scattered pages of a Filofax."

The precursor to rain, a slight chill in the air, was felt keenly by McCrystal and Bailey who were summoned late night to check the contents and confirmed that the items belonged to David Holden and should be returned to London with the body. Any shivers Youssef felt were due less to the drop in temperature and more to the fact that he had now found the piece of the kaleidoscopic jigsaw that confirmed Holden had got into the stolen Fiat after leaving the airport in the small hours of Wednesday December 7th. That, and the fact that he was withholding crucial evidence. The truth is that, among Holden's belongings left by the killers, Youssef had also found Holden's *British Petroleum* pocket diary. Acting on an intuition, he didn't log it but put the diary in his pocket without anyone noticing. He didn't know why he did this but a feeling inside told him that it might be wise.

It was a standard one-week-to-view diary large enough to write down quick appointments for each day, but small enough to be carried in a pocket. One page was missing, indicating to him that the killers were interested in this page only and didn't want the police to see it. Equally Youssef had to assume that the killers were deliberately showing them what they wanted them to see.

The missing page would have contained information for the week ending Saturday December 10th. The pages after this were for the most part blank, apart from simple reminders to send Christmas cards and buy presents for some relatives. Youssef was now only interested in the four days from Saturday December 3rd to Tuesday December 6th, with that last date being Holden's last full day before he was murdered. Up to Friday December 2nd, Holden had still been in Amman.

3pm Interview KH
9pm Meet KM – hotel

Youssef later learnt that the first line referred to Holden's interview with King Hussein, which everyone was aware of. And the second entry was a meeting with Kinza Murid later in the evening, a French reporter for "Nouvel Politique", a news magazine. Despite the fact that this page had not been removed and was therefore unlikely to have anything to do with Holden's death, there was a whole lot of noise breaking out around Murid, with Holden colleagues in the Sunday Times pressing him to interview her, saying she had stayed late in Holden's room. Youssef did not discount the possibility, but he knew that this detail was not important, he knew that the killers would have ripped out that page too had Murid had anything to do with Holden's death. Noise that only he knew to be a waste of time and energy! Youssef started to suspect that the killers might have the power to be playing them. He resolved to set down some traps, and this time he was not going to trust anyone.

6

On Thursday evening, the three units reconvened for a debrief, excited by the news of the car. The sexual angle had already reached a dead end, so Captain Mahmoud's team was disbanded and merged with Faisal's team to consider the crime as financially motivated. But even Faisal had become more convinced that the robbery angle was a dead end too. Everyone believed that Holden's was a political killing with an international dimension.

"Officers, listen up," began Faisal. "We now know the car Holden got into after he left the airport, so we need to go back to the airport and run interviews again, especially with those who were there on the night of the attack. Captain Mahmoud, your team will lead this. We also need to go to the car owner's neighbourhood, and to Al-Duqqi, to ask if anyone saw anything. This will be led by my team." Faisal looked towards Youssef who was listening but deep in thought. "Colonel Youssef, you might like to brief the team on the political angle?"

"Thank you. Officers, this crime remains most likely politically motivated, and there are strong indications that we are being played as well. Suggesting a significant amount of organisation." The meeting became quieter. "The owner of the stolen car is a Palestinian second-year university student, with an uncle connected to a known violent group, but this could be just a coincidence, or perhaps even a diversion."

"Surely our friends at Section 110 can make him talk?" said one of the officers to the laughter of a few; Section 110 being a division in the State Security Department known for using torture in interrogations. Keen to impress Youssef, they'd no doubt hoped that the colonel would like the nod to Nabbawi's iron fist. Youssef's predilection for such 'persuasive methods' had long been assumed by all but noted by none. Could the rumours be wrong?

"And I am sure they will get a confession too! But would it be believable? I think we should release the poor kid… but keep the car with us," Youssef said to the amazement and murmur of his colleagues and especially Major Faisal. "Yes, Major," Youssef said as he turned to look directly at Faisal. "I haven't gone soft, not yet anyway. There is truly no need to torture the kid, is there? You see, these killers are cleverer than all of us. The car was reported stolen by the owner on November 27th, exactly nine days before the murder… Why? Who would keep his own car with him for nine days after reporting it stolen, then use it later in a serious crime, only to release it back to us!"

"True, Colonel Youssef! Also, why steal a car so far ahead of time?" replied one of the officers.

"What's more is we know now that Holden left London to go to Damascus on Sunday November 27th, the same day that the car was stolen. This indicates careful pre-planning by his killers because, if you remember, at that point Holden planned to arrive in Cairo on Saturday December 3rd, before he decided to take a last-minute detour to the West Bank."

"You mean he was a target from the day he left London?"

"Indeed Major Faisal, and the ramifications of this are huge for us. It means the killers were watching Holden from London, well before he arrived here. From now on, officers, we will withdraw from any engagement with any foreigners in this investigation, especially the UK government and the Sunday Times. And who knows at this point who else is involved in this murder? So no one talks to any outsiders, even Egyptians, without my permission. Clear?" All present at the briefing shouted back that it was exactly that.

But Major Faisal had an additional question. "Colonel Youssef, if there is an international organisation involved, surely all the more reason to look into the Palestinian student, the car owner, and his flat mates; and his uncle who is linked to terrorism. Shouldn't we have at least investigated them first… before setting them free?"

"Again, think about it… if Palestinian extremists want to carry out a murder of this scale and complexity, and they need a stolen car, do you think they'd use one of their own? And why would they report it stolen six days before the murder? In fact, why would they even leave the car behind for us to find it?" Youssef's younger colleagues were visibly impressed by his logical thinking, clinging to every word like he was a schoolteacher-crush.

"And keep the car for one week after the murder too. Isn't that a huge risk to keep a stolen car used for murder for that period?" asked one of the officers.

"Exactly!" exclaimed Youssef as the officer blushed. "In fact, why leave the car at all? Officers, think about it, the car and the stuff we found could have easily been burnt and destroyed in the desert and no one would be any the wiser; but no, the car was left for us to find, and they waited one week after the murder to leave it there too… presumably the killers waited until they were sure they were in the clear. My guess is they're no longer in Egypt… gone!"

"But hang on Colonel, are you saying that they deliberately wanted us to see what they left in the car?"

"Most definitely, officer. It took them one week to sift through Holden's belongings, a whole week, officers, so what did they want us to see? They gave us his suitcase and some other sundry items, his papers and clothes and so on. What they gave us is the stuff that's not important to them." Youssef was careful not to mention the diary.

To the laughter and even amazement of others, one officer felt the need to summarise: "Colonel, maybe I'm not following, but it seems to me that you're saying we should not be led by what we see but by what we are *not* seeing!"

"Thank you, officer, well said indeed. But even what we are not seeing has been well orchestrated. For example, Holden's passport is still missing with the travellers' cheques. They probably want us to think that the motive is robbery. Who knows? We may find out more when we find the second car."

"Second car?! Do you think there will be a second car?" Faisal almost shouted.

"Yes, Major, my guess is we will. Notice two things about this car?" asked Youssef. Everyone was on tenterhooks. "First there is a lack of blood in the car, yet we know our victim was shot from the back and must have bled out; second the presence of an extra headrest which doesn't match the fabric of the other car seats."

"So they killed him in another car? That explains why this car was repainted… to make it look as good as new just to trick Holden into thinking that the drivers were respectable," added Major Faisal.

"Yes Major, I am glad you're now in agreement with me, but the extra headrest makes me wonder if it was left to us for a reason. We must keep an open mind, officers," concluded Colonel Youssef. And every single officer was sure those last words had been directed at him personally, such was the colonel's reach and their desire to please him.

By that time, Friday December 16th, the Mene House Peace Conference was in its closing stages. As if to upstage Sadat, the US President was meeting with Begin unilaterally, and the world's attention had well and truly shifted away from David Holden's suspicious death. Not only had Lebanese newspapers stopped reporting on the murder completely, even the Sunday Times had stopped reporting updates. This gave Youssef's team a breathing space to focus on hard criminal investigation. They reconvened their door-to-door enquiries and reinterviewed witnesses. But Youssef sensed the complexity. He knew he was dealing with a highly experienced organisation, probably an international intelligence outfit, and knew better than to let the killers dictate how this investigation would go.

He asked Major Faisal to clear one white wall in their office and position pictures to create a mental map. This was a new concept back in the 1970s and something that Faisal was not familiar with at all. Youssef had learnt it on one of his training courses in England. So, for Faisal and Mahmoud, moving images and words, arrows and question marks, around on the wall was quite a novelty… and they stayed all night long to get it finished.

Then they stepped back and surveyed the wall.

"Do you see it, Faisal?" Youssef asked and without waiting for Faisal to respond he continued anyway. "Everything points to what Holden was doing in the last 24 hours of his life, when he was not in Egypt. If we can establish his movements during that period, the chances are we can pin down his killers."

"How so Colonel?" asked Faisal, failing to see Youssef's point.

"The killers must have known exactly when Holden was coming here, yes?"

"Yes, obviously so."

"Then they must have also known his movements in the last 24 hours before he arrived. We should not care too much about the time before that for now, so… do we need to establish who knew when Holden was arriving in Cairo?"

"Yes, Colonel. And many people did, in fact." Faisal had now moved away from the wall to look at his personal notes. "Mr. Mustafa Amin, the editor of the newspaper Al-Goumhouriya, Mr. Christopher Wren of the New York Times in Cairo, Peter Kayser and Imad Jawhar of Reuters in Cairo… he may also have informed the British Ambassador Mr. William Morris and our new Minister of

Information, Abdul Monem Al-Sawwi," Faisal answered reading loudly from his notebook.

"No, Major, I mean yes, these people knew Holden was coming to Cairo for sure, and there are many others too. But I am talking about those who knew when exactly he boarded that 20:40 flight RJ503 in Amman. Remember, according to his colleagues, he changed his departure date twice, and even lost his hotel bookings in the process. There must be few people who knew that Holden was going to be on that particular plane. Otherwise can you imagine his killers hovering around the airport with a stolen car on the off-chance they might bump into him?" asked Youssef with some sarcasm.

"I see Colonel, I think you are right, so we must know who exactly he *did* tell about his rearranged flight. But..." Faisal scanned the wall again. "Why only the last 24 hours? Shouldn't we go back to the people he mixed with from the date he left London on November 27th?"

"No, Faisal. With Holden changing his flights at least twice, his killers in Egypt had to be sure that he had caught that particular flight. That could only have been the case when he had finally boarded."

"Or maybe, even, one of the killers boarded the flight with him! Just to be sure!" Faisal exclaimed.

"Exactly!" shouted Youssef. "That is very plausible. Faisal, did we check the names of all the passengers on the flight manifest?"

"Of course! And we traced them all... and interviewed every single one of them!"

*

Youssef now felt he was getting somewhere. And this feeling of progress intensified as he watched Faisal searching the flight manifest for a second time. All the names were written in two languages, English in accordance with international law, and Arabic in accordance with Egyptian law. Though the Arabic names were easy to follow and most of them were traced and accounted for, the foreign names were mostly tourists who came on a one-week holiday 'as a job lot' so to speak and left together too. Youssef noticed that the translations into Arabic of many of the foreign names varied between the visa application and the manifest. On checking with airport staff he was told that this was common since the exact spelling of foreign names in passports rarely matched the spelling on the plane ticket. Airline rules dictated that they should translate the English to match the passport and not the ticket in such cases.

A few foreign names caught Youssef's attention; one passenger in particular was translated into Arabic phonetically as "Lawrence", as in Lawrence of Arabia. He wasn't even sure if this passenger was male or female or even if it was a first or last name. But when he tried to match the name with the visa application, he found only one name that matched, in English written as Richard Shotel Lorenz, an American. He was part of a large group of forty American tourists from north-western Ohio on a tour to the Holy Land organised by a pastor called Reverend James Stewart in Fremont. Almost all of them confirmed that they crossed the Allenby Bridge from the West Bank and boarded the same flight, also taken by Holden.

Killers don't hang around longer than necessary, thought Youssef. And the ripping of the labels from the victim's clothes suggested they wanted his identity to be kept secret, at least for a short period, enough to allow them to flee the country safely. Faisal was given his new task: to list all the men who were on flight RJ503 but left Egypt shortly after, between 7th and 9th December.

- One American (Lebanese origin) businessman came on a business trip, left on Friday 9 December to London after a case of severe food poisoning.
- One Iranian student came in as a tourist but left with his brother on Thursday 8 December for Paris; the brother is a student in Egypt and their parents live in Paris.

- One East German, a mechanical engineer, came on a business trip but left for Aden in South Yemen on Friday 9 December; it's confirmed that he came to fix a problem with some machinery in a sweet factory in Helwan and left.
- Three Sudanese who were construction workers, working in Iraq, on their way to a holiday home via Amman and Cairo, they came together and left together for Khartoum on Thursday 8 December.
- One Tunisian student in the American University of Beirut who came to visit his cousin on his way back home and again both of them left together, the cousin is a student at Cairo University.
- Two Jordanian students who entered as tourists and both left next day on Friday 9 December for no apparent reason and seemingly without connections to Egypt.

Faisal's attention was of course drawn to the two Jordanian students who came and went after two days. *Who would come to Egypt for such a short tourist visit and go back to where they came from?* he thought. And students too! *Had they gone to another country we could say they used Cairo as transit but...* The major was still convinced that the key to Holden's murder had a Palestinian angle – either the rejectionists or the Israeli Mossad.

On the other hand, the colonel's attention was drawn to the East German engineer, who came from Amman but went to Aden after only two days. Youssef thought it very unlikely that Palestinian rejectionists would select Holden as a victim. He agreed that the Mossad were more likely to commit such an act, but knew the timing was all wrong for Israel to take such a risk during an historical peace conference. Despite Holden being critical of Israel's treatment of the Palestinians, there were many other journalists who were even more critical of Israel than he had been. And, above all, why bother with a journalist?

Further enquiries revealed that the two Jordanian students had come to Egypt to take back the coffin of their neighbour, another Jordanian student who had died in a car accident, and his elderly parents asked these two to bring his body back to be buried in Jordan. The sweet factory in Helwan also confirmed that the East German engineer had been genuinely required by them since the machinery was made, and only fully understood, in East Germany. The engineer had been on holiday in Jordan when they contacted his company to go to Cairo on his way back to Aden. Another dying lead… and it was time to brief the president again.

"Sit down, Youssef my son and tell me, have you got a result on the Holden case? I am getting more and more embarrassed trying to keep London sweet."

Nabbawi interjected: "We found the car, Your Excellency Mr. President, in which we believe Holden was taken from the airport."

"I know Nabbawi, you told me this before. Why then don't we have an arrest?"

"Your Excellency Mr. President, if you will permit me," said Youssef, knowing full well that Sadat wanted to listen to him anyway, "this is not our crime to solve… Ah, what I mean is that this crime has nothing to do with Egypt, it just happened to be committed in Cairo. It is for London to solve!"

"My son," it was Sadat's turn. "What you are saying is profound and rather overwhelming, so explain to me slowly, what do you mean the crime has nothing to do with our nation?"

"Your Excellency, we have a journalist who has upset many countries in the course of his work, but on the face of it not enough to eliminate him in this brutal way. The operation appears to be too complex for something so mundane… add to that the fact that there are many other journalists writing just the same stuff as Holden."

"That's true, what you are saying makes sense to me so far…" nodded Sadat. "But why? Why choose Cairo? Why not Amman, London, Damascus or even Jerusalem?"

"One of two things, Your Excellency." Youssef was on a roll! "First the peace conference might have been a diversion, or second, a simple case of logistics. If the former, then it means an intelligence outfit like the CIA or MI6 for example …" Youssef stopped at this point as he sensed he was probably divulging more than he should, and that Nabbawi would be annoyed.

"Or Mossad?" asked Sadat.

"Or the Mossad of course, Your Excellency Mr President, but do you think Mossad would risk doing something like this at a time like this? When their peace negotiators were on their way here? Imagine if we caught them in the act, or if Holden had managed to get away? The risk's too high for them to even contemplate this."

"Very good my son. Nabbawi, make sure you get all the help from the boys at the Intelligence Directorate," said Sadat as he dismissed the meeting.

"Youssef, son," said Nabbawi as they joined the motorcade back to the ministry. "I can't stall London any longer. Prepare yourself to go to England."

It hadn't been flannel! Youssef was genuinely convinced that the reason for killing Holden had nothing to do with Egypt, or even the Palestinians. The Sunday Times crowd were briefing them almost daily about who Holden had met in Amman, in the West Bank and Damascus. But Youssef regarded most of it as unhelpful noise. "More deafening noise," said Youssef to himself as he symbolically put his hands on his ears. "There is so much noise around this case! And it worries me." On the other hand he was impressed by the deadly silence of the actual killing operation itself, performed with the precision of a Swiss watchmaker. He half-joked to himself that if he ever succeeded in arresting the brains behind the murder he would congratulate them on a job well done.

Discipline, Youssef kept saying to himself. *That's the key.* No one saw Holden get into a car, no one saw the car being stolen nine days before or dumped one week after. Holden had simply become invisible after exchanging his $200 into Egyptian currency at the airport. That irked Youssef a great deal. He felt there was something he was missing, something hiding in plain sight.

With the leads drying up, the team briefing at the police HQ no longer topped and tailed the long working day. Now they only met in the morning. There had been no new leads; not until Monday December 26th, when Youssef had a phone call from Major Faisal. "Colonel, we found a second car, just like you said we would."

"With a missing headrest, right?"

"The very one, Colonel… But we didn't find it in Cairo. We found it in the city of Tanta!"

7

Youssef had always guessed that the murder itself was not carried out in the car they found in Al-Duqqi. Nagib's Fiat had only been used as the "abduction car". But he hadn't expected the second car to be found far away from Cairo. In a farming city like Tanta, located in the heart of the Nile delta, almost 100km north of the capital.

The second car was another Fiat Nasr 128, this time a 1974 model in its original green colour. And it was a government car! The registration number Gizah District 4213394 used by the Egyptian Ministry of Agriculture. It was a pool car used by a few employees in one section in the ministry. It too had been reported stolen, by the Ministry in fact, but unlike the first car, it was reported stolen on Tuesday morning December 6th; the same day Holden arrived in Cairo late at night. Sure enough they found blood stains on the front seats; it was a model of car that had front seats laid out as one continuous unit with no gap for the gear lever. They also found an empty cartridge case – matching the fatal 9mm bullet – in the rear passenger compartment. It looked to have come out of an automatic pistol with a silencer. A headrest was missing from one of the front seats, matching that found in the first car. Youssef and Faisal had finally found the "murder car". It too had been broken into via the quarter light window and then hotwired.

Youssef was suddenly knocked off balance by a hard-hitting wave of despondency and doubt. For the first time in his life, his ego had to bat off a touch of imposter syndrome. At the morning team briefing he looked mournfully at the depleted team; members had been pulled away from the team to work on newer, more pressing cases. So when he did address colleagues regarding the "murder car", the tone if not the words sounded like a resignation speech. "Like everything about this mad case, the more questions we answer the more questions spring up, but the picture is beginning to get clearer, more focused, now that the second car has been found. Still, there remains a sense that the killers are *giving* us the evidence they are willing to share with us. It just took us ages to find it! So this time they want us to know that this is the car where the murder was committed. There is some blood on the front seat. That, along with the marks on the body, show that Holden was dragged forcibly by his kidnappers and shoved into it. We have to assume that by then he must have guessed he was in mortal danger. He was shot from the back seat by a third person. The headrest of the front seat was removed so the shooter could get a clear and straight trajectory to the victim's heart from his shoulder." Youssef asked an officer on the front row to get up and act as the victim as he mimicked the killer's posture delivering the shot from the back, using his hand as the pistol.

"Is this the car that was used to take the victim to the Al-Azhar University Campus, where we found him?" asked Captain Mahmoud.

"Either that, or here is a third car tasked to do just that, to take the corpse and drop it off as just lying there. But my hunch is that this *is* the car, yes." Then Youssef continued, "But more importantly, ask yourselves, officers, a far more difficult question. Why are the killers so keen for us to see this evidence? Why keep a car for almost one month and then suddenly present it to us, with all the blood and the cartridge and the headrest too? Why not burn the car, or destroy it somehow, wouldn't that be neater? Officers?" Total silence fell in the room for a few moments.

"When was this second car reported stolen?" asked one of the team.

"Ah, thank you that man! That's also critical. It was reported stolen during the morning of December 6th, shortly after the victim checked out of his hotel in Jerusalem on his way to Amman Airport to catch his flight to Cairo. It may indicate that someone in Jerusalem had signalled to the killers here to steal this second car ready for the murder."

The meeting ended with the usual hum of opinions being voiced, a few saying deliberately loudly that it seemed clear the Palestinians had a hand in it, whilst Mossad was also mentioned more than once as officers left the room. Youssef, Faisal and Mahmoud remained there, staring at the mental map on the white wall. The three men were sunk deep in thought. Silence reigned.

Suddenly, Youssef seemed back on form. He punched one hand into the other, muscles tensing as he did so and stretching the crisp shirt. "Gentlemen, let us take stock of what we have here…" Faisal and Mahmoud waited for Youssef's discerning insights. "We are now all assuming that this operation was, one, executed by an international agency operating in Egypt, and two, well planned and organised with high precision." Faisal and Mahmoud nodded their agreement.

"But there is a number three!" said Youssef rather loudly and his colleagues looked puzzled, hoping he wasn't about to ask them what it was. "Three, the killers want to manipulate this investigation and steer us in a particular way, which means we may have spies among us!"

In the face of silence, Youssef turned to the white wall for inspiration and started annotating while he spoke. "Having completed their gruesome deed, the killers have been keen to show us the evidence of their crime, but obviously only what they want us to see. It is as if they are interacting with us. Officers, we need to know more about how the local police force dealt with locating these two cars, from the days they were reported missing to the days we were informed about them. To whom were the cars reported stolen? And how did they know to contact us …? How did they guess that these two cars might be connected to the Holden case?" Just as Youssef was scanning his officers' faces and thanking his lucky stars he hadn't gone into the teaching profession, Faisal had a eureka moment too.

"So, they're killing two birds with one stone, steering our investigation in the direction they want us to go, and at the same time checking what other evidence we have when we report it to the press! That must be it!" Mahmoud, feeling left behind somewhat, thought it was important for him to speak too:

"But this is a basic criminal investigation technique. We only ever report to the press certain pieces of information, to see how the perpetrator reacts."

"But the difference here, Captain, is that the killers are leaving us a trail and they want us to follow it," answered Faisal.

"But hang on," said Mahmoud. "If this is the case then the killers too must have blind spots regarding what *we* know… surely? They cannot possibly know everything we know. It's blind spots all round!" Mahmoud wondered if his colleagues would understand the point he was making. Youssef offered to elucidate.

"Yes, timing is an important dimension in this investigation, and we must look at the timing of the evidence being found too, not just the evidence itself."

"So the time when each piece of evidence appeared to us is in itself *evidence!*" Faisal shouted the last three syllables to his colleagues.

"Exactly! Throughout this investigation, every time we hit a dead end or got conflicting information, what happened…? The killers gave us a large piece of evidence to chew on. We must consider the timing of everything in this investigation… everything!"

Mahmoud started writing a series of steps as a timeline on the wall. 'Step one, Holden takes a plane from London Heathrow to Damascus on Sunday November 27th. At the same time the "abduction car" gets stolen here in Cairo. Implication: the killers know that Holden has made a move from London and is on his way here." He wrote as he spoke. "Step two: wait!" Youssef and Faisal looked startled. "I mean literally, wait. They waited, they didn't need to steal another car yet, not until Tuesday December 6th when Holden checked out of his hotel in Jerusalem. Maybe at that point, when they stole the first car, they only wanted to abduct him, to rough him up, maybe they didn't want to kill him. The decision to kill was not taken then, but later, perhaps on Tuesday 6th December when they stole the "murder car". This would imply that something happened during Holden's trip from Damascus to here that made them decide that their operation should be upgraded from abduction to liquidation, which is step three." Mahmoud wrote his last sentence quickly and waved his hand as if he was an artist adding his signature.

"Someone in the West Bank or Amman gave the signal to London and Cairo to move from Plan A for Abduction, to Plan L for Liquidation, and the killers in Cairo were in place ready for either," Faisal continued.

"And then came step four, December 7th: they gave us a body, admittedly unidentified at first, early morning on the outskirts of Central Cairo. They could have lost the body in the desert if they'd wished, or made the body harder to identify, allowing the actual killers time to flee the country, but instead the foot soldiers, the operatives, stayed behind in Cairo and had more work to do."

"Which means that their work in Cairo is not yet finished! Which means controlling our investigations was part of their plan too!" declared Mahmoud. Youssef smiled watching his two colleagues exude the same energy he'd been feeling all along.

"And step five, gentlemen," Youssef continued, taking the marker pen from Mahmoud. "When the killers saw us as units divided between money angles and sexual angles and getting nowhere, they pointed us back towards the political by giving us the first car, the "abduction car", complete with Holden's personal effects." Youssef's next words took on a hushed tone. "Yes, officers, the killers are with us, watching us. They know exactly what is going on here! As if they are talking to us!"

"Sir, what benefit's to be had from steering us back to the truth? Why not let us continue thinking it was a robbery or a sexual murder?" said Faisal.

"Because," Youssef was unshakeable, "the real culprits want us to go down a certain route. It's a message."

"A message to us?" asked Mahmoud.

"Possibly, but not necessarily. It may be a message from one intelligence outfit to another for all we know right now," answered Youssef. "Yes, I am sure of it, these are messages from one intelligence agency to another, and guess what, we were and still are the inadvertent messengers! How stupid we have been! Middlemen!" Youssef jettisoned the board marker at speed, leaving Faisal and Mahmoud in awe of their colleague's drop the mic moment.

"But for us to go back and check the timing of each piece of evidence would be a huge task for our exhausted team, Colonel Youssef," Faisal said rather despondently.

"There might be a simpler way," answered Youssef. "Going directly to the killers' den and talking to them. Guys, it's time I took Nabbawi up on that trip to London."

8

Heathrow was as grey and rain soaked as Cairo had been when Colonel Nabil Youssef landed there on December 28th, but a great deal colder. At least that was to be expected. On the flight with him was the body of David Holden, released to its final resting place.

It had been tough, leaving Saira and the baby. All that warm, new life left behind to investigate a cold-blooded murder with even colder strangers, probably. Smug strangers they'd be no doubt… *showing me, the Egyptian policeman, how to be a proper detective.* Youssef thought this on the surface, probably because he thought he should expect this. But he was completely self-assured, he was hoping to exchange ideas and best practice with Scotland Yard. Just the words "Scotland" and "Yard" conjured up visions of Sherlock Holmes for Youssef. He'd read those adventures in Arabic during his early teenage years, avidly.

At odds with the macabre cargo, everyone was still in a festive Christmas mood: life has an innate habit of carrying on. Youssef was told that he'd meet with Scotland Yard's Chief Superintendent Raymond Snell and Detective Chief Inspector Sam Campbell. He added to his itinerary a visit to Holden's colleagues at the Sunday Times. Perhaps he would even meet with Ruth Holden, the widow, to pay his respects. Youssef was actually looking forward to what London held in store. On landing, he put his hand in his pocket to check that his wife's long list of presents that needed buying was still there. He'd promised her the latest Western kitchen gadgets, beauty products, music cassette tapes and some soft toys for the baby. Actually the list was endless. But time wasn't. His sudden anxiety over his domestic to-do list started to seep into his professional psyche: *What if there's another murder in Cairo while I'm away?* he thought to himself. *What if the killers have a list too… of more targets needing bullets?*

*

Youssef was not an idealist. He knew his country had limitations like any other. And that these limitations were very Egyptian! His elder brother was killed fighting Israel near Ismailia in 1969 during the War of Attrition that followed the Six-Days War. They never saw their brother's body; he was presumed dead, with full honour. So chaotic was Egypt in those days, the Egyptian Army wasn't even sure where his brother was at the time he was killed. Their presumption of death came from the simple fact that the Ministry of War in Cairo didn't receive his application for his annual leave on the due date. The army then sent their father a letter with the full name of his soldier son and a verse from the Quran, "Think not of those who are slain in Allah's way as dead. Nay, they live, finding their sustenance in the presence of their Lord; They rejoice in the bounty provided by Allah". He remembered with pain how his father collapsed when he received that letter. How his mother was inconsolable. She still sometimes hoped he might be alive, perhaps a prisoner of war in Israel or living in Europe as a deserter. One day Youssef visited the front where his brother's unit was based and couldn't believe the daily humiliation Israel's bombardment inflicted on his compatriots. He saw that their enemy was fighting to live while the Egyptians were fighting to die. Youssef even flirted with the thought that, somehow, they deserved the consequences of their mistaken engagement in the war. Sadat was right. As painful as it was to admit, Youssef saw that it was right to be offering the Israelis peace at last.

But just as he'd started coming to terms with Egypt making peace with Israel, he gets asked to investigate the murder of a British journalist who seems to have understood the Arab perspective of the struggle with Israel so well. That was something which made him uncomfortable. It didn't sit well with the narrative he and his brother had grown up believing in either: that it was the "British" who were responsible for the making of Israel, for taking Palestine from the Ottomans and giving it to the Jews. He recalled the saying from school: "the one who didn't own gave it to the one who didn't deserve it". The caustic humour behind that summation made him think of a line he'd read in a New York Times article about the Mene House Peace Conference: an American delegate, noting the bonhomie that existed between the Israelis and their hosts, joked that Jews and Muslims were calling each other by their Christian names! So, to be investigating the murder of a British journalist sympathetic to the Palestinian cause seemed anomalous.

*

Needless to say, Youssef's head was all over the place as he landed at Heathrow. And a brisk walk to *Arrivals* later it was about to start juggling with something else that felt awkward to him: Detective Chief Inspector Sam Campbell of Scotland Yard, who was extending her hand to him in front of the London taxi ranks, was a woman! He knew the 1970s was progressive, even more so in Europe, but he hadn't expected gender equality in a police force. He didn't know how to deal with the situation at first, coming close to asking her if Chief Superintendent Snell was about. But Youssef warmed quickly to Campbell. She was entirely professional, yet very open too, naturally inviting confidence. She looked directly into his eyes as they spoke, something that Youssef felt very aware of without quite knowing why he was struck by it.

They had to wait until Holden's coffin was brought down from the plane, before leaving for the coroner's office at St. Pancras. Still at the airport, Youssef had paid his respects to Ruth Holden and the few of the Sunday Times colleagues who had stayed behind in London during the seasonal shutdown and arrived to pay their respects to Holden's body. First stop after that was the hotel that had been booked for the colonel, where Campbell waited for him to drop his stuff in his room. Then together they went to meet Chief Superintendent Snell at the Yard.

It was a difficult meeting in many ways, partly due to the language barrier. Youssef had learned English at school and found it frustrating that his accent, which he thought he was eliminating rather well, wasn't clearly understood by Snell and Campbell. Almost every sentence had to be checked twice to make sure they understood it correctly. Combine that with the need they felt to dance around the issues of the murder investigation and try to get what they needed from each other, without giving too much away, and you have a meeting impressive only in its formality and superficiality.

"I will have to leave you with Campbell here, who I am sure will look after you well while you are with us." Snell was clearly not intending to figure in any more cooperation! "Please excuse me," he explained. "I am resuming my New Year's holiday at home. I wish you, Colonel Youssef, every success with your endeavours. .... Ah, I almost forgot, the Sunday Times crowd, watch out not to tell them anything they don't need to know. They need to understand the difference between a police murder investigation and investigative journalism. Pass my regards to Minister Nabbawi." With that Snell disappeared from their view.

Of course, neither Campbell nor Snell knew that Youssef had his own agenda while visiting London. Yes, he was keeping Sadat and Nabbawi happy and yes, he was attempting to keep the British on side with his presence. But the overriding purpose of his visit as far as he and his team were concerned was to check if their own investigation had been breached, and if it was being manipulated from London rather than Cairo.

Snell and Campbell hadn't shown him any signs of knowing what was going on, so he decided to visit the Sunday Times the next day, Thursday December 29th. Campbell went with him. They found the offices at 192 Gray's Inn Road to be seasonally decorated but practically empty due to the Christmas break. Just a skeleton staff working there, several of whom Youssef had met briefly at the airport. The person who took charge of his visit was Paul Eddy who was the editor's assistant. He took Youssef around and introduced him to their editor Harold Evans where they all sat in his office. Youssef gave them the same brief he gave the Yard. But they were clearly more frustrated at the pace of progress than the Yard were. Youssef even detected a sign of some resentment from them at the way the investigation was going but he pretended not to notice. Eddy kept telling Youssef how Holden was sympathetic to the Arab cause, and enthusiastic about the peace with Israel, as if this applied moral pressure on the Egyptians to solve the murder mystery. But then they asked Youssef why it took so long to identify Holden's body. Youssef took this as an opportunity to flip the script. "May I ask why it took the Sunday Times three days to raise the alarm about Holden going missing? Especially when Holden, as we now know, was so punctilious about informing you of his movements every step of the way?" There were a few unhelpful, embarrassed mumbles. Then Paul Eddy answered:

"Well, yes, it was a bit remiss on our part, but Holden had been on many visits to the Middle East before, even during the war, and come back safely. We hardly thought he needed nannying during a time of peace. But yeah, we are sorry we didn't raise the alarm sooner."

"But Paul, remember we thought at first he might have been quarantined for cholera?" someone in the room called out.

Youssef asked for translations of a range of articles Holden had published, particularly the recent ones. He wanted to ascertain whether there were any sensitive subjects Holden might inadvertently have ventured into. But it was getting near lunchtime, and they suggested a nearby Lebanese restaurant. No doubt Eddy thought that maybe this serious but charmingly handsome Egyptian detective would be more willing to confide in them with some familiar food and drink on the table.

In the restaurant that lunchtime were Harold Evans, Paul Eddy, Paul Hillman and Selena Cotton, all just back from their Middle East posts for the New Year. After a meal, wine and a smoke, Evans gave a short speech welcoming Youssef followed by reminiscences of Holden. By then, all tongues were loosening gradually. They started talking about the investigation again, going over all theories, possibilities and scenarios, and all the whys and wherefores that had plagued the investigation, in both countries, from the start. It was then that Youssef's subterfuge with the hidden diary got him a surprise result.

*

Youssef's idea for setting traps, or subterfuge, came from his fascination with an old puzzle his father once described through a folk tale when he was a child. He had used a similar principle in many of his investigations – feeding each person around him with a different piece of near-truth information, stressing each one not to divulge it, and then waiting to see from where he would hear a particular version back, thereby identifying the leak. So, taking Holden's diary to his office, he at once set about deciding on the various versions of misinformation he could share with each of his colleagues.

In Cairo, Youssef had spoken to each of his colleagues individually and told them that he'd become aware of Holden having an appointment to see a 'someone' on Wednesday December 7th at 3pm, which explained Holden's rush to catch this particular flight to Cairo. Youssef told them that they must not tell anyone and that he was going to check with the president's office to see if this information checked out. That 'someone' was identified as a different person in each conversation. Youssef told Faisal that the 'someone' was Abdul Monem Al-Sawwi, the Minister for Information. To Mahmoud, Youssef said it was Morsi Sa'ad Al-Din, Director General at the Ministry of Information. And so as to know if the minister's office could be a source of a leak, Youssef told Nabbawi that the 'someone' was Musa Sabri, editor at the Al-Akhbar newspaper. Youssef made a note in his notebook of the names. All he had to do now was wait.

*

Youssef had expected that he would hear one of the fake versions from someone in Egypt. He didn't. He actually heard it from the Sunday Times crowd in that Lebanese restaurant in London.

"Did you manage to interview Mr. Morsi Sa'ad Al-Din yet, Colonel?" It was Harold Evans, the editor-in chief-asking the question, probably in an attempt to show off his inside knowledge and wrong-foot Youssef. "Apparently he had a 3pm appointment with Holden on Wednesday December 7th. Maybe he knows something?" Youssef experienced a surge in adrenalin but had to control his responses before anyone noticed anything. He never expected this! Captain Mahmoud of all people was the source of the leak… And in communication with London! He knew it didn't mean there was anything sinister in Evans' knowing about this, as he may have heard it second or third hand, but the source of this misinformation was Captain Mahmoud without a doubt. He felt in his guts that he was dealing with the complex murder of a mysterious man, with international links everywhere. The game has become dangerous. *I have to be careful now*, he thought.

"Oh, that came to nothing," Youssef shrugged the question off and changed the subject. "I was planning to go to Paris and meet Kinza Murid, but I see that I am pressed for time… and I promised my wife some gifts. Is there a Marks and Spencer anywhere near us?" Youssef didn't mind them thinking that he was lazy or incompetent, as Westerners would think that about him anyway. He had what he wanted and was in no hurry to answer more questions.

The next day took on the shape of a traditional investigation when Youssef and Campbell went back to Heathrow, to meet with the member of cabin crew who had served the section where Holden was sitting in flight RJ503. Her name was Nicki Webster. Initially Youssef planned to meet Webster alone, ask her a few questions, but Campbell warned him that he did not have jurisdiction to carry out witness interviews in London and it would compromise both the investigations: Cairo and London. On the face of it, it didn't seem to matter much. Youssef already trusted Campbell and in any case Webster claimed not to remember Holden, or anyone else for that matter.

But there was a secret in the diary that Youssef did keep solely to himself. On the inside back cover of Holden's 'British Petroleum' diary, there was a short cryptic note most likely written by Holden himself. Youssef thought the killers might have missed this note, or might have left it deliberately, but whatever the case may be, he still thought it may have some significance and wanted to look into it. The note was written, or scribbled rather, with a shaking hand and some of the letters were a little broken, as if someone was writing it in transit… maybe on a plane that was going through turbulence or coming into land. The note said:

Must explain later to HE not to worry about the note to NW on RJ503.

Youssef thought that Holden may have been in a hurry when he wrote the note. But when he later made an enquiry with the Royal Jordanian Airlines, Youssef learnt that the name of the air hostess who served Holden's section was Nicki Webster. He guessed that "NW" must mean her. Youssef had already sent a request to Scotland Yard to interview all RJ503 crew members as a matter of course, well before he saw the note. When he went through the report sent back via the British Embassy, it said that Miss Webster was on a long-haul flight to the United States and they had to wait for her to return to the UK before the Yard could speak to her.

What Youssef struggled with was who "HE" referred to. Most likely it was a person's initials, or it could have been an abbreviated title like His Excellency. Youssef had made a list of all of Holden's family, friends and colleagues and "HE" fitted only one person: Harold Evans. Holden had perhaps given a note to Nicki Webster and felt he needed to remind himself that he had to explain something about it later to his boss. So he wrote a quick reminder in his diary during his flight. How these two names could be connected was a mystery. But since Harold Evans had already shown he knew a concocted fact, Youssef had reason to conclude that the Sunday Times crew knew more than they were letting on regarding the investigation.

Youssef decided not to ask Evans or Miss Webster if they knew each other or whether they knew anything about a note being written by Holden. Instead he cut his London visit short, thanked everyone for their warm hospitality and took the next flight back to Cairo. It was New Year's Eve. He'd not found time to buy the presents he'd promised Saira. His brain was racked with tormenting, conflicting thoughts, none more tormenting that the unwelcome sexual attraction he felt to Sam Campbell. Tired and mentally exhausted, no sooner had he boarded his plane and found his seat than Youssef crashed out thinking to himself, so much to do, so much to go through, so little time.

Drifting between consciousness and lucid dream, he effortlessly created his own version of flight RJ503…

9

For David Holden, the chaos of Amman Airport always conjured up images of the aftermath of the 1967 Six Days War. There was something about such chaos that attracted him, something innocent and guileless in this superficial disorder at a time when such disorder was not to be tolerated in Western airports. Chaos in Western airports, when it happens, is a reaction to a failed system; yet in Arab airports, chaos is the system. Back in the 1960s, to kill waiting time, Holden travelled a great deal and he used to amuse himself by watching people at airports, especially in Middle East cities, trying to guess what would happen next. He waged bets with himself... Who would manage to check in before who? Which flight would take off before the one that was meant to? He even developed an antenna, almost psychic, for the Arab sense of how things are done. He felt the rhythm of their daily life, and he liked it. He talked about it in his book 'Chronicles of Arabia' about how oil changed Arabia, the one many Englishmen were fascinated with, forever. Holden was not pro-Arab, far from it, he didn't care for the social double standards, the treatment of women; but he sympathised with their causes. He was always interested in how the post-colonial policies of the Allies after World War Two affected normal family life at the lowest levels in the Arab world. He'd developed a skill in writing about this in his articles. So, when he came to the airport in just-about-enough-time for his 20:40 flight to Cairo, he checked his flight on the newly installed Solari display board in the airport lounge. Flight RJ503 to Cairo had just "flapped" running on time, as scheduled. He had enough time to write a few notes in his diary about who he'd just met and what his impressions were. It was difficult to believe early that morning he had been in East Jerusalem, was now in Amman, and that in a couple of hours he would arrive in Cairo. The wonders of modern travel *he thought!* Then a Royal Jordanian employee came into the departure lounge shouting: "Calling passengers for Flight RJ503 to Cairo, please proceed to the Gate number 3".

The plane was a Boeing 727, the one with the narrow body, that Royal Jordanian Airlines had recently added to their fleet. The passenger area in the fuselage was split with one aisle in the middle and two three-seat bays on each side. The flight was almost full and there was no first class, so everyone was equal. Holden didn't mind that at all, as long as he arrived in Cairo on time. The only thing that he cared about was being allocated an aisle seat, which 26C was. He didn't like to be squeezed between two people and, as it was a night flight, over a desert, sitting next to a window had little value. In the ritual scramble for the seats as they embarked, Holden found himself sitting among an American tourist group and saw that his neighbours, sitting next to him in the same row, were a middle-aged couple. They looked familiar to him somehow; he thought he had seen them before but wasn't quite sure. The woman sat in seat 26B next to Holden and her husband was by the window.

Holden had an innate dislike for all things American, as was common for his generation, even though he'd studied for his M.Ed in Illinois in the early 1950s. The American woman, in her late fifties, was friendly and chatty, which Holden wouldn't normally mind. But he needed peace and quiet to process the many events that had taken place that day, and the day before too, in East Jerusalem.

"It is indeed a cold night, nearly freezing they were saying just now. I didn't expect it to be that cold in this part of the world," said the American woman. Holden, pretending to be busy reading a newspaper, looked around to acknowledge her; then, out of politeness, he responded:

"Yes, it's a desert, it always gets very cold after sunset." Holden hoped the unintended sarcasm would put an end to the uninvited small talk.

"Oh, my name is Mrs Barbera Bonnette, from Clyde, Illinois," she said to Holden who, out of courtesy to a fellow passenger, had no option but to reciprocate.

"David Holden" he answered briefly and reluctantly.

"We've just been visiting the Church of the Nativity in Bethlehem, thought we'd go visit Cairo since we came all the way here," said Bonnette. "I think we might have seen you in the old city in Jerusalem yesterday Mr. Holden. If I am not mistaken you were buying souvenirs with your friend." Holden felt nervous at this point, as if he was being watched. But Bonnette looked very ordinary and genuine, perhaps this was just a coincidence.

"Yes, I was there ... on business." Holden thought she'd be less likely to pursue a conversation with someone travelling on business than a fellow fun-seeking tourist, but he was wrong.

"And what business are you in Mr. Holden?" asked Bonnette.

"Oh… I am … a writer. On Islamic history," said Holden thinking that it would be better to say that than that he was a journalist, to stop her talking about religious Christian stuff all the way to Cairo, as he gathered they were in a group from the same church on a pilgrimage to the Holy Land.

"Oh, that's great, then you must have been to Cairo before? This will be our first time and we don't know what we have in store for us there... perhaps you can suggest some places?" said Bonnette much to the annoyance of Holden who now was hoping that this distracting small talk would be over soon, and not stop him from thinking.

"But that's absurd! How can anyone plan to visit Cairo without knowing what they will see there?" Holden's curt answer to his neighbour was intentional, a signal that he was not interested in more dialogue. Bonnette, taken aback by his answer, more or less left Holden alone after that.

Less than half an hour into the three-hour flight, a blonde English-looking hostess brought a passenger from the back rows and waved him into seat 25D. It was an aisle seat like Holden's, one row in front. Holden was trying to catch some sleep during the flight, a little anxious that his hotel booking at the Meridien might have been lost in the confusion of him changing his itinerary last minute. He was also exhausted after his long day in the West Bank, and so didn't notice the man at first. But later he noticed him constantly turning his head, looking at him, intently, with a fixed look. He was Middle Eastern in appearance. Holden didn't think him Egyptian at first, more Jordanian or Palestinian. He was tall with a thick moustache and still wearing his unusually thick, fully buttoned-up fur coat – unusual for an airplane passenger, even though it was cold that night. The man kept turning his head pretending he was looking for someone at the back, but smiled at Holden every time they made eye contact. Another passenger to annoy and unsettle the hapless Sunday Times journalist. Initially Holden thought the man was another busybody like Bonnette, trying to strike a conversation to pass the time, but there was something about him he didn't trust.

Holden decided to test if he was watching him or not by going to the bathroom. As Holden exited the cubicle, sure enough the man was standing in the galley, waiting for him.

"Mr. David? Yes?"

"Yes, sorry have we met? I thought your face looked familiar," answered Holden and shook the hand in front of him. Holden was used to Arabs calling people by their first name.

Ignoring Holden's question, the man then said, "My name is Besuouni Abdulsalam Amin, from the Egyptian Presidential Special Guards. I thought you might want to know that the President would like to meet you, to ask you to conduct a one-to-one interview with him and get you to change your mind about Egypt… get you to know the real Egypt."

"Sounds like a great honour… but I'll have to inform the newspaper first. No doubt they'll be thrilled. But forgive me, may I see your ID? Unusual for an Egyptian official like you to make this request on a Jordanian plane!"

Amin produced a badge with an eagle emblem and Arabic script. "I am not here in an official capacity, but we will meet you when we land in Egypt. Just thought I'd take the opportunity to explain to you in advance."

"That's fine, and of course I would be delighted to interview the President," answered Holden.

"Excellent, I will meet you with my colleagues after we land in Cairo Airport, in the baggage reclaim area, we can arrange the date and time of the interview with the President then," said Amin and moved as if to go back to his seat. But then he added, "Oh, by the way, it may be quicker for you if you don't say you are a journalist when you fill in your details at the airport, just say something else, otherwise our Ministry of Information will whisk you away through their system and it will delay you and us."

"One minute… can I ask … how did you know it was me? I mean you don't know me, right?"

"Oh, we know you Mr. David, this is not the first time you have come to Egypt," answered Amin.

Holden nodded in politeness but was unconvinced by Amin's answer. Regardless, he was excited that this might be his lucky break.

He knew that the New York Times weekly magazine was trying to get him to interview Sadat but the request had been declined, most likely because it was an American magazine. After his visit to Jerusalem, only a few had managed to get an exclusive interview with Sadat. It looked like Holden was about to scoop an historic interview to add to his string of exclusives, like the one he had just finished with King Hussein. I must let Harold Evans know... I will telex him from whichever hotel I end up in, *he thought to himself.*

On his return to his seat, the American woman, Bonnette, asked him something but Holden wasn't even listening, he simply ignored her. Amin had disappeared. It was now well over two-thirds into the flight and suddenly Holden started to feel nervous. There was something not right going on around him: an American couple who happened to have seen him in Jerusalem the day before sitting next to him, and an unknown man springing from nowhere offering him an interview with President Sadat. Why would an Egyptian working in the Presidential Guards travel on a Jordanian airline? What did the man mean when he said to 'get you to change your mind about Egypt' and 'this was not the first time he'd been to Egypt'? Holden had not been that critical about Egypt in his articles, and it was almost a decade since Holden had been to Egypt, Nasser's Egypt. He started to feel uneasy about the whole thing.

But Holden didn't feel he was in any danger, just uneasiness about something not fitting quite right. Of course, if anyone attempted anything suspicious, he could always resort to basic human instincts, shout for help! He'd done that before, many times in fact. Nonetheless, as an insurance, Holden decided to write a simple note. He had a small piece of paper and a pen in the inside pocket of his jacket. He took them out carefully and started writing. He didn't know what to say exactly or to whom he should write. Then the English air hostess came into his eyeline, Nicki Webster her badge said. She sounded like a northerner, a Geordie even, like him. Had to be trustworthy! So

Holden wrote on the small piece of paper:

Dear Nicki: my name is David Holden, I am a British journalist, if you hear of anything bad happening to me in the news, in the next few days, then I kindly request that you, or your airline, contact Mr. Harold Evans at the Sunday Times in London (Tel: London 01 837 1234 Ext 7275) and tell him that I was approached mid-flight by an Egyptian man with the name Besuouni Abdulsalam Amin, asking me to interview Sadat - Thank you. Flight RJ503, 6th Dec '77.

Holden then did something more daring. He waited until Nicki Webster came to serve some drinks to the passengers near him and slipped the note into the pocket of her waistcoat without her noticing. Holden thought that this precautionary action was needed. He didn't want to alarm Webster with such a strange note or even explain it to her during the flight, she might tell others and cause a situation. He thought it better to leave her to find the note later when she got to her hotel. If his fears turned out to be unfounded then Webster would ignore the note, but if his fears had some basis and something bad did happen to him, something that would be reported on the news, then the message might be crucial. *She seems like a decent woman, thought Holden as he dozed,* and if it turns out to be a false alarm then she'll have a story to tell at dinner parties.

10

Holden's plane touched down in Cairo at exactly 23:12 local time. The temperature was a little above freezing, but felt much colder. He was wearing his corduroy suit and polo neck sweater which were just about right, yet he still felt the chill in the air. The American couple who had followed him as he disembarked finally disappeared from his view; they'd found their travel agent waiting for them before they reached passport control. But the other man he'd met, Amin, was nowhere to be seen. Holden wondered if he'd been the subject of a hoax or prank and strangely enough almost felt relieved.

The arriving passengers then started down the old terrazzo floor of the dreary wide corridors of Cairo Airport to arrive at the same old chaos of passport control. Palm-sized visa application forms were filled in by new arrivals waiting in the queue – easier for those traveling in groups as they had backs to lean on – one third of the form required English and the other two thirds Arabic. The form was formatted for Arabic script, from right to left, and the English translation of each question was written tagged on like an afterthought. Holden was used to filling in these forms; he put down his hotel as the Meridien which was the booking he believed he had. When he got to "occupation" he hesitated for one second and then put "writer" just as Amin had suggested. Holden said to himself, what's the worst thing that could happen? *Strictly speaking he wasn't lying anyway, he was actually on a sabbatical from his employer writing a book about Saudi Arabia.* Maybe Amin will turn out to be genuine and I can meet him without the fuss of the Egyptian Ministry of Information *he thought. But Holden did lie about one thing: when he got to "Purpose of Your Visit" he put down "visit". Writing "business" would raise more questions and have him end up at the Ministry of Information anyway.*

This probably cost him his life, thought the drowsing Youssef. *Had he told the truth, that he was a journalist covering the Peace Conference, he would have been whisked away by the Ministry from the airport and transported to his hotel, alive!*

When his turn finally arrived, Holden handed the visa application form to passport control. The immigration officer looked at him and mumbled something about payment for visa being due on arrival and that it had to be exact cash with no change given. Holden knew that this was a tactic for illicitly bribing passport control officers. He handed over a $50 travellers' cheque adding "you can keep the change". The officer responded with a loud stamp on one clean page of the passport. It was exactly 23:38 at that point.

"Welcome to Egypt Mr. David," the officer said.

His red Samsonite suitcase was conspicuously waiting for him at the baggage reclaim area, but not Amin. There was however another man. He too was wearing a thick coat, but also had a Russian style headdress, a shapka, covering his ears and most of his face. He was standing so close to the red case that Holden had to address him.

"A'an Iznak" He remembered from his old days in Egypt that this meant "excuse me".

"You must be Mr. David, yes? Mr Besuouni Abdulsalam Amin asked me to wait for you here to give you his contact details." The man handed Holden a business card with an eagle emblem and printed names and numbers, some numbers having been scribbled on by hand, as if corrected, with a blue ink. Holden was impressed with the stranger's English; he spoke clearly without the distinctive Egyptian accent.

"But Amin promised to meet me here," Holden responded.

"Oh yes, he is here Mr. David. It's just that he's waiting outside. He had to go outside to meet someone. I'm Abdou, by the way…" the man answered as he extended his hand. "Is there anyone else meeting you here? Did you book a taxi?" asked Abdou.

"No, I didn't arrange anything actually… everything was last minute," answered Holden.

"Then please allow us the honour of giving you a lift to your hotel Mr. David… it is late now… difficult to find a decent taxi in Cairo… Our car is parked in the long-term parking zone. A little walk, but not too far. And it would be a pleasure."

"Fine but I need to exchange some money first if you don't mind," said Holden.

"Sure, go ahead. You will see me waiting outside in the foyer just behind that door," answered a gesturing Abdou.

The exchange of money took Holden just a few minutes, then he left the baggage hall and entered the airport foyer. This time Abdou behaved as if he were a taxi driver and started to walk a few steps ahead of Holden leading him to the car he'd mentioned. They left the airport foyer from one of the side doors, not the larger main one at the front. Abdou was courteous to Holden all the way. He took his suitcase from him and continued walking ahead, crossing the taxi rank towards a large rectangular unpaved area which was under construction but well-lit and comfortable enough to walk on.

A short distance later they came to another unpaved area where the lighting was dimmer and the airport terminal building seemed suddenly much further away; the hubbub of the airport no longer audible. Instead the chirping of insects could be heard, loudly. Holden started to feel a little uneasy as far fewer people were around. But Abdou kept reassuring him, pointing to a car in the distance. "This is Mr Amin's car!"

The car was a green Fiat Nasr, make 128, registration Gizah District 421339. It looked decent and nearly new. He could even make out Amin sitting in the rear seat, just behind the vacant passenger seat. In fact, he thought it strange that Amin didn't get out the car to greet him, instead shouting out some words in broken English on how he'd managed to get out of the plane faster than him... something to do with being an Egyptian VIP. Abdou put the suitcase in the boot of the car, asked Holden if he wanted to put his briefcase there too, but Holden waved that he wanted to keep his briefcase with him, and then the door to the front passenger seat was opened for him to get in.

Holden hesitated. It felt to him as if they were expecting him to join them there and then, and that was not the deal he had agreed with Amin in the plane. The car looked more like a taxi than a VIP car used by Presidential Guards. Something was amiss, but it was too late for Holden to back out. Instead, he determined to give them the slip on arrival at the Meridien should they turn out to be sinister.

Holden placed himself in the front passenger seat and the driver, who didn't look at him or utter a word, not even a greeting, pulled away gently. But as soon as they had left the airport area, the car started to speed up, especially when they joined Salah Salem Street towards the east. The conversation also gradually started to get stranger. Shifting from small talk about the weather, all the niceties, to passive and then active aggression.

'So Mr. David, why do you British journalists always write lies about Egypt?" Amin asked Holden.

"Oh, not all journalists my friend! Many write the truth. The problem is that truth is often an elusive thing, Mr Amin. You know that!"

There were now fewer cars on the road. But at least the driver was driving in the right direction, towards the hotel; he recognised some of the landmarks, despite the many years that had elapsed since his last visit to Cairo. Holden's mildly reassuring observations were obliterated in one fell swerve as they reached the back of the Al-Azhar University compound. They almost spun into the abandoned wasteland there. It was a surprisingly secluded area considering how close it was to central Cairo. There the car stopped.

Amin, sitting directly behind him, grabbed Holden's neck with the full length of his arm as if to choke him, rendering the Englishman immobile. Abdou then pulled the headrest of Holden's seat, took from his pocket a silenced 9mm automatic pistol, and shot Holden from the back with a single bullet just above his left shoulder. Holden's body started to shake, one of his hands tried first to punch the driver, then Amin in the back seat, but within a matter of seconds he was still. His heart had stopped. Holden died within less than a minute of the pistol being fired. It was fast and it was efficient. The journalist's life had been snuffed out within half an hour of his leaving the airport, at 1.38am on Wednesday 7th December 1977.

Immediately after, the driver and Abdou, in the cover of darkness, lifted Holden's body out of the car and laid him in wasteland along the main road. They stripped his pockets, cut out all labels from his clothing, and vanished. The corpse was left at the side of the road. There was no second car; there was only one car. The "abduction" and the "murder" car was one and the same.

*

Youssef's plane begins its descent, but he is still dreaming. As if he doesn't want to miss the end of his subconscious revelations.

*

It's 2:13 am, Garden City, Cairo, the HQ of the Secret Presidential Guards Unit for the Protection of the First Lady. Captain Besuouni Abdulsalam Amin enters the commander's office and places the eliminated journalist's passport on the desk. The commander sees something unexpected in the photo and takes a closer look.

"This is his passport?"

"Absolutely sir," he said. "Mission, as they say, accomplished."

"You utter, utter idiot!" *The commander shouted.* "This isn't David Hudson … You've killed the wrong man! This is a disaster! A disaster! What are we going to say to Her Excellency?" *The commander is phoning the Head of the Presidential Guards Unit for advice as he speaks.*

"The President and the First Lady have no idea about this operation, we kept it away from them," *comes the advice on the other end of the line.* "Let them find out what's happened like the rest of the world. Hide the man's belongings well and we'll tell you later what to do with them."

Five hours later, Sadat and the First Lady, Jehanne, are sitting in the garden having breakfast; Sadat wearing his camel-skin Arab robe as it's a particularly cold morning. The phone rings for the First Lady. She goes to take the call. After three minutes she returns to her husband.

"Is everything alright Jehanne dear?" *asks Sadat.*

"Yes darling, everything is fine."

*

Youssef shook himself free from his dream as his plane landed. It took him a few seconds to process where he was and that what he had experienced was just a lucid dream, no matter how "real-seeming".

At the airport, Minister Nabbawi was the first to meet with him.

"We may have a mole among us, Your Excellency. I mean one

operating at an international level," Youssef told him in a rush.

"Really? Well, don't worry! Leave that to Major Faisal to run with. Your white wall and your showboating... not to mention your constantly interrupting me... has paid off!" Nabbawi smiled to show he was in a jovial mood. "His Excellency the President wants you... yes, you Youssef... as the new head of the Presidential Guards Unit."

PART 2

11

London, Saturday December 17, 1977 (ten days after Holden's murder)

"It seems they are digging up the road again… a Christmas present for us maybe… and it's only the third time this year. Or is it the fourth now?" Sam Campbell was drinking her tea and turned her eyes from the window of their Muswell Hill flat to her husband who was sitting reading the morning newspapers. "Um, are you with me, darling?" asked Sam.

"Hmm, yes, I know, hopeless," answered her husband Stephen, lifting his head briefly, and then continuing with the papers. "Hey, look here… there's something about your new case in the paper! The Holden case, tragic… How are you moving along with it?"

"You know I can't tell you much plus we only just got the case. Snell has applied for jurisdiction for me to go to Egypt to lead our own investigation there and hopefully teach the Egyptians what to do and what not to do!"

"Oh, you do get all the fun!" Stephen said sarcastically as Sam summoned up a smile in return and went back to looking at the omnipresent roadworks from the window.

The Campbells had been married for eight years with no children: she, a second wife to him; he, her first husband. They had fallen in love at work where Stephen was superintendent and Sam had recently been promoted to DCI. One of the first female DCIs in Scotland Yard's history actually. They had lived in their flat for six years and witnessed many "land shifts" on the road outside it; one service company after another, digging and re-digging, sometimes 'just in case', until Sam thought they must be running job training schemes along their road. But it didn't much matter during the week when the couple were out working.

Sam had climbed the ladder to the accompaniment of much sexist name calling. Especially from her female colleagues. She didn't care, not much anyway. It had been a long time since the first women were recruited by the police force. It took two world wars, and a bit more, until the Sex Discrimination Act was promulgated. Male defenders of a now-ancient empire had been railroaded into focusing hard on how they acted when women were present; changes to how they addressed their female colleagues was still a long way off.

On Monday December 19th, Campbell went to work as usual. It had been eight days since the brutal killing of David Holden in Cairo became known to them. Many influential people had been shaken by the seemingly senseless murder of a decent British journalist. The word on the street was that Holden was not particularly an establishment man, in fact at times he was more the opposite. But he was an upright and respectable crafter of words and adroit with sharp wit when it was called for. He was, after all, an Englishman.

It shouldn't have come as a surprise to DCI Campbell that she was allocated the Holden case. She was known to have outstanding capabilities when it came to solving political murders. In the early 1970s, London had become a theatre of assassinations by various international groups, mainly the IRA. The open feel to the city, the changes in visa rules allowing overseas students to come in without careful vetting, and the expansion of rapid long-haul jet travel to and from Heathrow allowed for easier movement of people, and this included assassins. Her first case had been the 1971 attempted murder of Zaid Al-Rifai, the then Jordanian Ambassador. Rifai, known for his strong opposition to Palestinian warfare in Jordanian territories, had only been slightly wounded, but he was to remain a target after Jordan's Black September troubles in 1970.

Many cases headed Campbell's way after that. Like her investigation into Teddy Sieff's attempted assassination in 1973; the chairman of Marks and Spencer. Then came an actual murder, this time an IRA hit that killed the Irish political campaigner Ross McWhirter. Campbell had managed to identify the perpetrators of all these crimes, whether they were caught or not. Yet the Prime Minister Edward Heath at that time insisted that these sporadic crimes be treated as local crimes. Campbell tried her best to emphasise the context of these politically motivated crimes. What was the point of catching brain-washed monkeys, when the organ grinders were thousands of miles away? No one appreciated Campbell's views in calling for setting up a unit for political international crimes, except Chief Superintendent Raymond Snell, her boss at the Yard. When the massacre at the 1972 Summer Olympics in Munich shook the world, Heath finally yielded and agreed that a police unit dedicated to these political crimes was required.

But when the Yard assigned Sam Campbell the investigation of David Holden's apparent assassination in Cairo, she was puzzled. Investigating a crime that took place in London was one thing, but a crime that took place in a different country? A non-European one at that. Well, that was another. How could she investigate a crime thousands of miles away from her base, almost five days after it took place? So when Snell rang her on December 11th, she asked him about the logic of it all.

"You do know that the most critical evidence is collected in the first 24 hours? How do we know that the Egyptians aren't busy covering it all up?"

"I know you Campbell, remember! You can sniff out irregularities and inconsistencies. Don't let me down, Sam. A whole lot hinges on this case."

Those dreaded last words, about not letting a boss down! What hinges on what, exactly? How many times had she heard that cliché? Yet in her experience, every time she came close to the truth of a crime the "hinge" seemed to slide somewhere else. Ever since Henry Kissinger brought the spirit of Realpolitik to the West, the "art of the possible", if it can be called an art, looked more like "appeasement", a licence to commit murder. *Don't upset the Soviet Union! Tread carefully with that dictator!* So much for pragmatics. It wasn't that Campbell opposed the new spirit of openness with the communist bloc; far from it, she was wholeheartedly for it; Western powers have not been entirely innocent either with their covert interventions in Africa and Latin America. But Campbell was also an ardent defender of the truth. The uncoated version. Not the one trimmed and bound to "not upset certain governments". So, used to clashes with her kow-towing superiors, when she met her boss Snell on Monday, she asked him the same again.

"But you will have a lot to go on before the body even arrives in London, go see the grieving widow and the man's stunned colleagues at the Sunday Times. Build your case, my dear. Find out what sort of man Holden was."

"You mean babysit them all, guv?"

"Look Campbell, Merlyn Rees told us that the new Egyptian Interior Minister, General Mohamed Nabbawi Ismail, promised full openness and cooperation – give them the benefit of the doubt. Nabbawi confirmed in his letter to Rees that for their part, they have appointed a star team to investigate this murder." Then he lifted a copy of the letter from his desk and said, "including a colonel. Nabil Hassan Ali Youssef... his name... You know... all this reminds me of my time in Egypt during the war..."

"But I am worried about the way the Egyptian investigators are leading this guv. They're even asking us who the beneficiaries of Holden's will are! As if his wife in England might have been behind his death in Cairo!"

"But aren't these the sorts of questions we ask? Isn't this what you asked Rifai when you first took the case? Let them ask all these questions, Campbell, be fair," said Snell.

"I did, of course I did, but that was when... oh, never mind!" sighed Campbell in the end.

"Look, the body will be arriving any day now, you will then have plenty to go on. But until then, go meet the widow, since you mentioned her, and visit his colleagues at the Sunday Times too."

Holden's family home was in Cannonbury, Islington; a leafy suburb of London. Campbell knocked on the door, feeling a little nervous for some reason. The door opened after few seconds, a middle-aged woman stood there.

"Good afternoon, I'm Detective Chief Inspector Sam Campbell. Is this where Mrs. Holden lives, Ruth Holden?"

"She is inside resting, yes. I'm her sister. Are you with the police? I'm not sure she can cope with any visitors right now..." A voice from inside the house called out to the contrary and the sister waved to Campbell to go through a narrow corridor around a staircase and then into a front room, surprisingly quiet considering the noise from the road outside. The room was a kind of a studio with photographs displayed on the walls, wildlife photographs and also some portraits of famous people she recognised. Ruth, wearing dark clothes and dark glasses entered the room, shook hands, and sat in the chair opposite the one offered to Sam. Campbell offered her condolences.

"Mrs. Holden, I am trying to build a picture of your husband David. Would you mind describing him to me?"

Ruth hesitated. "But I already gave the police a photograph," she answered.

"Sorry, I didn't mean a photograph. I mean to describe him as a person."

"He's... or was... a wonderful person, sensitive... deep, thoughtful, that's in a nutshell who Dave was, detective. Did you read his obituary in the Sunday Times?" Ruth pushed an open newspaper in front of her, as Campbell nodded. "That article described Dave accurately."

"I need to ask a sensitive question, Mrs. Holden. Did your husband... Dave... have any enemies you can think of, who might harm him? Could be personal or work or people he wrote about..."

"On a personal level he was a wonderful husband and a real family man; a very private person. Like all Geordies he had a dry sense of humour, and had no enemies on a personal level, to my knowledge. But he was a journalist at a high-profile newspaper read across the world. He dealt with sensitive political issues and so the answer is I suppose 'who knows?'" Campbell was impressed with her answer. Ruth added, "I am a journalist myself as you probably know, a photo-journalist in fact. I too work with Dave at the Sunday Times by the way, but I work on ladies' fashion mainly." Campbell turned her head to look again at the photos on the walls, this time with implied permission. "Oh those are old ones, some I took myself when I was working with Life magazine. I was their London rep for many years." Campbell was by then looking at a Christmas postcard on the table, wondering why it was there when all the Christmas decorations and cards had been, understandably, removed from the room. Ruth noticed Campbell looking at the card on the table.

"This is the last thing David wrote to me, a Christmas card from Jerusalem. We were looking forward to spending Christmas at my parents' house in the country. Dave loved the English countryside even in the winter." Ruth handed the card to Campbell. It showed a sketch of an Arab street trader in Jerusalem, standing on a narrow street corner surrounded by tourists. On the back of the card, Holden had written:

Missing my darling wife in a city which may soon see a (long-overdue) peace.

"As you can see," she added, "like all of his generation, he was formal in everything he did and said."

On a deep level, Sam Campbell and Ruth Holden didn't quite hit it off. It was a chemistry "thing", or lack of it, between them. Also, they were different "types" of women. The best the DCI managed to throw together with regard to fashion was a pair of jeans and baggy top combo. In fact, Campbell had avoided formal occasions all her life, just to avoid wearing a formal dress. She felt she didn't look right in them. Ruth also didn't think much of Campbell, she thought she was a victim of a masculine society that requires women to behave like men to succeed. She wasn't keen on those women and regarded them as mere victims and mostly unintelligent. Ruth's brand of feminism was that women should set their own agenda, not imitate their male counterparts.

"By the way," Ruth said. ".. You might like to speak to David's elder brother too, his name is Reginald. He is a solicitor working in Essex. He can give you more details about Dave, from his childhood and life … before we got married I mean. He is the only surviving member of the Holden family now." Campbell agreed to do exactly that! She believed that the most difficult crimes were solved more quickly by fully understanding the victim first. She took down the contact details from Ruth, arranged a meeting with him on the very same day and went directly to Liverpool Street Station to catch the next train to Colchester, where Reginald Holden was working.

They met in the train station's coffee shop. Reginald was naturally upset about his "baby brother", there were only the two of them in the family. Despite the age difference of five years the two were close and had remained so till the unexpected end. But they were different too. Reginald was a more conventional type of character, taking after their mother. David was very much like the father, a pathfinder, a wannabe pioneer: "David regarded our dad as his role model, he practically walked in his steps." The father was Thomas Shipley Holden, the name Shipley being from the grandmother's side. Thomas was a well-known local journalist, the son of a local printer himself, who later became the editor of the Sunderland Echo, a local paper with a good circulation in the region.

"Dad encouraged both of us to get into journalism, but David was the more gifted one. From an early age actually. He was always witty with words and insightful in his analysis from the get go. He had so much still to give."

Reginald shared with Campbell how they'd both lived together in a nice suburb of Sunderland, proud Wearsiders, what with the football and all. "It comes as a package when you are a northerner," he said. But David was also a sensitive man. He learnt music at an early age and played the clarinet. "This talent came from a great uncle from my father's side, William. He had a local orchestra of his own and travelled everywhere around Durham with it."

What was surprising for Campbell to learn was that David had early on pursued a career in acting, even trying his luck in Hollywood. First he'd studied geography at Cambridge. After some interruption due to the war, he graduated in 1947. While Reginald had joined the RAF after the war, David had won a fellowship to study in the USA, at the Northwestern University in Illinois. This was where the idea of Hollywood was born, but Reginald couldn't remember exactly who had influenced David to take up a career in acting.

At the end of her meeting with Reginald, Campbell felt a certain attachment to her victim; she was beginning to understand him. Above all she admired his interest in why people didn't see things in the same way. This always fascinated her and she sensed this might have cost him his life, but wasn't sure how. It seemed to her that Holden was interested in areas where there were seismic differences in opinion over the same issue, he had spent his best days chasing areas of conflict around the world, never fearful of stating what he believed. He was only 22 when he wrote his first serious article, in his dad's Sunderland Echo in 1946, just after the war. It had centered on the troubles in Palestine before the state of Israel was even created! Later this became his area of expertise, the Middle East conundrum. *A martyr for a cause maybe,* thought Campbell.

His 1946 article "Problem of Palestine – Causes of the Present Troubles and a Suggested Remedy" was a visionary solution to the Palestinian problem, for its time. To be a visionary so young is one thing, but to be a clairvoyant? The article was published on July 16th, one week before the terrorist attack on the King David's Hotel in Jerusalem. An attack authorised by Begin, the incumbent prime minister of Israel, and his paramilitary force. Many British personnel were killed in that attack and British opinion was inflamed by it.

"Crimes of violence by Palestinian Zionists recently aroused feelings in Britain far from conducive to clear thinking," was how Holden had opened his article; and the brief overview of the history of Palestine and the two-horse strategy adopted by the British during the First World War ran true to his open-minded empathic approach. He didn't run shy of the facts that Britain had promised Zionists a national home in Palestine; to secure Jewish financial funding for the World War One; and promised the Sharif of Mecca Arab independence over the whole of Syria, which in his thinking included Palestine. His article suggested that the root cause of the Arab-Jew conflict was economic; two communities having been allowed to develop separately at different paces in the same the country. The Jews, he argued, were advanced farmers, yet the Arabs were farmers of poorly watered soils. The end of Turkish rule and the conscription to its army meant the Arab population in Palestine had grown beyond their subsistence levels. The 1936 Arab uprising was a result of this economic disparity. Holden's visionary solution was to call for a change in British policies to allow the two communities to live in one merged state with similar standards of living. He certainly had all the ingredients needed to become a successful journalist and social commentator, which was exactly what he set out to be.

12

The next day, Chief Superintendent Raymond Snell spoke to Campbell in his office first thing. "They'll soon be flying the body to Heathrow and there will be someone from the Egyptian police coming with it, the same man I mentioned to you, a Colonel Youssef. Also some journalist from the Sunday Times. Better inform Mrs. Holden… even if they've already told her it had better come from us too."

"Excuse the nod to protocol, but surely an official inquest's needed, yes? We must open one immediately before this investigation can officially go ahead."

"Of course! But I detect some energy in the way you're requesting this, Campbell. You're not usually this procedural!"

"Forgive my emotion guv. This investigation is becoming more and more like a media circus. We seem to learn more from newspapers than the other way round… in fact we're chasing them, begging them to share their sources of information with us. You might as well appoint John Knight as the official investigator …"

"Who's John Knight? Oh, you mean the Sunday Mirror man? Are you talking about his article today?" Snell showed her the newspaper.

"This journalist seems to have full access to the Egyptian investigation team! He even published a photo of the crime scene, or wherever Holden was found, and also a car!"

"A car? Which car?"

"I rest my case!" Campbell tried to regain her composure. "Apparently the Egyptians found a car with Holden's personal effects inside it, did you not read that bit?" She took the newspaper from Snell and showed him the photo of the car printed on a later page.

"I see, hmm… make sure we claim it! I mean the personal effects not the car obviously. It's within our rights to do so, and everything should be logged in our evidence room too, as part of your investigation."

"Absolutely guv, but you can see where the problem is. John Knight is openly discussing various theories in a national newspaper. He's talking to everyone in Jordan and Israel and has men on the ground in Egypt. We have no chance on finding the truth from…"

"Use them!" Snell said loudly.

"Guv?"

"Listen, Campbell, journalists thrive on information, its value and its timing, nothing else. They also have difficulties controlling their childish imaginations. But in Holden's case this can be useful. You should be experienced enough to sift through the information and filter the facts from the fiction, surely? So do it!"

She did it, by swallowing her pride and principles and setting up a meeting with Holden's boss, the editor of the Sunday Times, Harold Evans. Campbell knew that, since the Kim Philby affair, the relationship between the British establishment and the newspapers was strained and clouded by suspicion and mistrust. The journalistic desire to beat all competitors and break any piece of news first was always a driving force. As long as a newspaper had a source, reliable or near enough, they would print first and check later. The dailies relied on the short span memories of their readership and banked on not being sued for misinformation. But the Sunday Times was a weekly, and more analytical. The DCI understood the difference well.

At first, Campbell was asked to wait outside Evans' office. She watched him through a glass wall sitting with his staff around him. Evans was making all sort of gestures to his team: she recognised Frank Giles and Paul Eddy from a past case, among a swarm of others all trying to get noticed by the editor-in-chief.

"Please come in Chief Detective Campbell, Mr. Evans is free now," said Evans' secretary and waved her inside. Evans was standing ready to shake hands.

"Chief Detective, sorry to have made you wait. It's bloody crazy around here right now, sadly due to the Holden case... anyway please take a seat. I have just been on the phone with the Chief Super." Evans explained how the Sunday Times had decided to assemble a team of investigative journalists: the ex-Insight editor John Bailey and Cal McCrystal in Cairo, Paul Eddy in Amman, Paul Hillman (already in Amman), Anthony Terry, a war hero but known to have worked for British intelligence, in Jerusalem, and Selena Cotton in Beirut. "Their task is to retrace Holden's steps in his final days," Evans concluded.

What a lesson! Campbell resolved there and then to not listen to her prejudices. She found Evans charming, impressive, and as engaging a man as she'd ever met. "Mr Evans," she found her voice. "I came to ask you to cooperate with us." Evans was surprised. He thought they already were.

A detailed discussion between the two followed. "We must work together to nail whoever the bastards were that killed our man," said Evans. Campbell agreed. But when she requested that any information the Sunday Times receive come to her first, the two had their first disagreement.

"Chief Detective, we survive on getting good information ahead of others!"

"You just told me you want to help us find those who killed Holden. You can help by drawing a clearer line between murder investigation and investigative journalism." Evans floundered about for an answer, taken aback by Campbell's directness.

He took a deep breath. "Please try to understand how difficult it is for us too, when you have a paper like the Sunday Mirror writing all sorts of wild stories about one of our own, and we cannot even respond."

The two came together eventually with a working arrangement on how to handle information received and on how to agree what was publishable so that the Sunday Times didn't look to be withholding facts from its readers. Then Campbell asked Evans, "Can I get a copy of all the telexes relating to Holden during his new assignment with your paper?"

Evans promised to get her all the copies she asked for. Campbell then asked to interview the man with whom Holden had spent the last week of his life in the Middle East, Edward Mortimer, who was with the Times newspaper, the daily one. This Evans arranged.

Mortimer appeared much younger than the DCI had expected. He was in his thirties, almost 20 years younger than Holden himself. A Modern History graduate from Oxford, Mortimer had already built enough expertise in the politics of the Muslim world to get him noticed. He was calm, almost boring with the details he shared, but he gave Campbell a great insight into recent Middle Eastern politics. "I was with David for a good part of what turned out to be his last week of life; we bumped into each other by chance on the last Tuesday in November, in Damascus. He had arrived only two days before. I tagged along with him and another American journalist, Wilbur G. Landry, an old friend of Holden from the days of the Suez Crisis, and the three of us travelled together by taxi from Damascus to Amman on Thursday December 1st. We were staying at different hotels at that time because we'd already made our own arrangements. Then, on a whim, Dave and I decided to go the West Bank, so we waited for the Allenby Bridge to be opened by the Israelis after the Sabbath and then went together to Jerusalem on the Sunday, checking into the American Colony Hotel." Seeing Campbell's inquisitive look, he added, "Don't be deceived by the name; its American roots go back to New England's puritanism hence it's a very austere place. It used to be an Ottoman mansion built outside the old city walls. Anyway, we spent most of Sunday and all of Monday interviewing Arab notables and mayors in the occupied West Bank. On Tuesday, Holden's last day if you like to call it that, we spent a few hours early morning walking in Jerusalem's Old City before we departed from each other, and he left alone by taxi to Amman airport to catch his flight to Cairo."

"And how well did you know Holden, Mr. Mortimer?" asked Campbell.

"Not that well to be honest, not before we met in Damascus, but during the last few days we spent together, we got to know each other more. We're from different generations as you know. Hey, would you believe we were never meant to meet in the first place?!" Mortimer was suddenly animated. "I was just standing in for Robert Fisk as the Times' Middle East correspondent, when the Sadat initiative came up. So in Fisk's absence, I had to go to the Middle East and report from there, otherwise I'd normally write leaders from London… in fact I rarely get to travel these days."

"How did Holden seem to you? What were your impressions of him?" asked Campbell, sticking to what was relevant.

"Wonderful companion! Full of anecdotes. The whole time in the taxi, from Damascus to Amman, he kept us entertained with his encounters and knowledge about almost every place we passed. Once we came across Turkish pilgrims coming back from Mecca, so he talked about Turkey and Ataturk. Then we went through Deraa by the Syrian border, and he told us about T.E. Lawrence's incident there. Sometime ago, he had apparently asked an old chief of the Bani Bakr tribe if he remembered Lawrence… the chief said, after thinking a moment, "Ah, yes, Lawrence, the man with the gold." He'd then turned to us and said "I never pass through Deraa without wondering whether Lawrence was, or was not, buggered by the Turkish commander..."

Campbell asked how he received the news of Holden's death. "Well, after we went our separate ways, on Friday December 9th, I got a call from the Sunday Times in London, asking me if I knew where Holden was. I said I thought he was in Cairo. They were worried because he'd normally have sent at least a one-line telex message saying where he was staying and what his plans were. But they hadn't heard from him at all. So I went down to the taxi office near the Damascus Gate in Jerusalem and spoke to the same taxi driver, Suleiman Rabi, who confirmed to me that he had taken David back to his hotel in Amman and dropped him there."

"And then?" asked Campbell.

"Then I didn't give it much further thought until the Sunday morning, a couple of days later, when I listened to the English news bulletin on Kol Israel radio. The lead item was "chief foreign correspondent at the Sunday Times murdered in Cairo". I felt sick to the stomach. A man I had spent such a wonderful time with a few days before, dead and in this way! A couple of days later, I flew to Cairo on the first direct civilian flight to make the historical journey from Tel Aviv. A day or two after that, the other Sunday Times journalists, John Bailey and Cal McCrystal, arrived too. Their mission was not to cover the peace talks, that was just their cover. They were there to find out what happened to David. I stayed at the Jolly Hotel at Gizah close by Mene House where the Peace Conference was."

"And, Mr. Mortimer, the Egyptian police? Did they interview anyone? Did they approach you?" asked Campbell.

"Absolutely. I was interviewed by the Egyptian police. They asked me to go over in detail all that I could remember of the time I spent with Holden in the West Bank. But they gave me the impression they were more interested in the reactions of the Palestinian political movers and shakers to Sadat's peace initiative than in who had killed David." Then Mortimer added, "Can I ask? Have you ever thought of going there yourself? I mean to Egypt? To see the crime scene?"

"I wish I could! We're still waiting for the jurisdiction paperwork to come through from Cairo…"

"Forget all that nonsense, they'll never grant it, but nothing to stop you going there is there? I mean as a tourist, or even as an undercover journalist. Who would know?" Campbell was surprised by the suggestion, it never occurred to her, but she thought the idea might have its merits. She didn't know how to answer. Mortimer then added, "Tell me if you ever decide to go, I can get you in touch with someone there and save you time. She's a lady journalist too and a discreet one."

"Thank you," said Campbell. "I might take you up on that offer."

Campbell saw no moral problem in disguising herself as a journalist or tourist in Egypt. It would be like the undercover work she'd had at the beginning of her career.

Mortimer asked if he could leave for another meeting. "By the way," was his parting shot. "Have you met Jan Morris yet? I suggest you do if you haven't, she and Holden were very close colleagues and friends."

13

Despite her reminding them, Campbell couldn't get copies of the telexes she requested from the Sunday Times. This alone made her more suspicious. Of course, she could request them from the Post Office, their local telex exchange, but that would be like looking for a needle in a haystack. She managed to piece together Holden's final movements from meeting Mortimer and others at the paper. This is what she recorded in her notebook:

Sunday 27 November, Holden promises the Sunday Times to cover the peace initiative and to write an article for the New York Times about it, takes the Syrian Arab Airline Flight No. RB408 at 15:00 hours to arrive in Damascus at 22:30 and checks into the Meridien Hotel. He has tickets from different airlines, one from London to Damascus, another from Amman to Cairo and the final leg from Cairo to London. Which means he always planned to go from Damascus to Amman by taxi. At this point his plan is to arrive at Cairo on Saturday 3 December.

Monday 28 November, in Damascus, Holden files his article "Cairo's New Miracle Offer" on Sadat's invitation to hold peace negotiations in Cairo, following his visit to Israel. It contains a provocative hint. A move which "put the Arabs, Israelis, Russians, Americans and Palestinians on the spot".

Tuesday 29 November, still in Damascus, attends a press conference given by Syrian President Hafiz Al-Assad which relays nothing unexpected except that a new rejectionist front is being formed to counteract Sadat's peace initiative. Holden spends time writing up his next article. He meets Edward Mortimer at this point by chance.

Wednesday 30 November, while in Damascus, suddenly it was announced that King Hussein of Jordan would be giving a press conference in Amman the next day at noon, and that journalists must arrive at the palace by 10am on that day. Holden sends a message to London that he's going to Amman by taxi and still aiming to arrive in Cairo, from Amman, on Saturday 3 December as planned. Also sends a postcard to his wife saying he will be going to Amman tomorrow. At this point, Holden doesn't plan to go with Edward Mortimer to Amman.

Thursday 1 December, early morning and on the move by taxi from Damascus to Amman, with the American journalist Wilbur G. Landry. But, last minute, Edward Mortimer asks to join them in the taxi. On arrival in Amman, Holden checks in alone to the Intercontinental Hotel, room 701, and later all three attend King Hussein's press conference as planned. The others then go to their respective hotels. It was clear to almost all journalists at the conference that King Hussein knew Holden well, almost like a friend of the family. Holden sends a message to the Sunday Times that he will file a new story in Cairo when he arrives on Saturday 3 December but, for the first time, hints he's thinking of possibly delaying his trip to Cairo to allow him to go to the West Bank for a couple of days. This is after Mortimer told Holden that he was going there himself. Holden asks for his reservation in Cairo to be either with the Hilton or Meridien but favours the Meridien.

Friday 2 December, in Amman, a public holiday, hence nothing much happened. Holden has lunch with Wilbur G. Landry and a few other American journalists. This is the date when Holden definitely decides to go to the West Bank but has to wait for travel agents to open the next day and for the Allenby Bridge to open on Sunday. Holden sends his article to the

Sunday Times, which he wrote when he was in Damascus, headed "Peace May Break Out After All" stating in it "though the dove of peace flutters hesitantly over the Middle East, more importantly the "hard-line" Arabs still have not shot it down". Also, later in the day, Holden and Kinza Murid are seen spending time together, ending with dinner in the hotel coffee shop and then moving to his room but "nothing" happens between them according to his colleagues as Holden was devoted to his wife. Murid is a young correspondent for Le Nouvel Politique a weekly French political magazine, similar to Time magazine.

Saturday 3 December, still in Amman, this is the original date that Holden was supposed to go Cairo. He spends the day mostly working on his article from his room, goes to the travel agency in the hotel to change his flight and then sends a message to the Sunday Times saying he will go to the West Bank tomorrow after all, but "for only one or two days." He is now planning to reach Cairo on Tuesday 6 or Wednesday 7 December, and asks them to contact Cairo hotels and inform them of the change of plans. This is the most definitive confirmation that he has changed his date for arriving in Cairo.

Sunday 4 December, on the move in the morning by taxi from Amman to Jerusalem via the Allenby Bridge crossing, this time with Edward Mortimer only, using a taxi from a company called Middle East Taxi Services. On arrival in Jerusalem both check in at the American Colony Hotel in East Jerusalem around lunchtime. The taxi driver's name was Suleiman Rabi. Holden takes a urine sample from a friend in Jordan and hands it in at Hadassah Hospital between 3 to 4pm immediately after his arrival, must follow up on this strange request, some say it belonged to a British journalist who didn't trust the Jordanian laboratories. Holden and Mortimer meet a few Palestinian mayors and journalists to gauge the mood regarding Sadat's peace initiative. After a long day, they are both tired and decide to call an early night knowing they have a full schedule tomorrow.

Monday 5 December, Holden and Mortimer in Jerusalem. Holden books a taxi for 8am and goes with Mortimer to see Bethlehem mayor Elias Freij. Mortimer recalls the meeting where Freij tells them "there is no such thing as American imperialism". Holden describes Freij afterwards, as "one of nature's moderates". Next they go to the Church of the Nativity. Next Holden visits the Tomb of the Patriarch, and then a souvenir shop. In the afternoon, Holden tells Mortimer that he's going alone for a walk in the Old City. On his return, both buy more stuff and go to an Israeli settlement, Kiryat Arba, to look around, then return to the American Colony Hotel. At the hotel, Holden meets the British Consul General, the Palestinian equivalent of the British ambassador. In the evening, Holden goes to the Christian town of Ramallah to meet Mayor Karim Khalaf who supposedly gave Holden a petition or memorandum requesting Sadat oppose the peace initiative. Then back to the hotel.

Tuesday 6 December, sends a Christmas card to his wife, which Ruth showed me when I visited her, and a postcard to Jan Morris, who I must interview and get to read what the card says. Holden and Mortimer go for a quick walk early morning in the Old City and then Holden checks out from the hotel around 8am, has the same taxi driver waiting for him to take him back to Amman. Mortimer sees him off at the Damascus Gate of the city around 10am. It is announced that an Israeli peace delegation would go to Cairo for talks starting on Monday 12 December. Holden decides to go back across the bridge and catch his ill-fated flight from Amman to Cairo, so he can be in good time to write a scene-setting piece for the Sunday Times for the coming weekend. Mortimer decides to stay a bit longer in the West Bank and visit Israel, particularly since US Secretary of State Cyrus Vance is about to arrive there. And this is when the two finally part. Harold Evans states that their enquiries from Amman seem to suggest that Holden went to the Meridien Hotel in Amman to pick up his bags which he leaves with them then goes to the travel agency in the hotel, most likely to check his bookings, and is seen talking to the elderly couple, archaeologists and friends of King Hussein, John and Isobel Fistere. But I must verify this.

Campbell felt she had established a good timeline in the run up to Holden's murder, albeit based on second or third hand accounts. *This will help us when we try stitching it together with the Egyptian findings later,* she thought. But a few things stood out to her already:

first how the idea of changing the itinerary and the detour to go to the West Bank came about, which Holden seemed to have decided to do off the cuff and last minute. It seemed that idea came when Mortimer told him he was planning to go to Jerusalem to meet some Palestinian politicians. Holden supposedly said he hadn't been to the West Bank since the Six Day War in 1967 and was attracted to the idea of meeting his old contacts there, for some reason. It was also a logical move since his remit was to study wider reactions to Sadat's peace initiative, and the West Bank reaction was crucial. Second, the timing. When Holden decided to go to the West Bank he was at first hesitant but his final decision came on Friday 2 December. If Holden was the victim of the deadly machinations of an international agency, as many predicted, then the murderers in Cairo must have been made aware of his last-minute change of plans. So, if an assassination team was deployed to Egypt by a foreign agency, it must also have been delayed for a few days waiting for Holden to arrive. Campbell made a note: ask the Egyptians to check who arrived before 3 December and did nothing except wait.

14

Jan Morris, an historian and a mountaineer, was still married to her wife with whom she'd had four children as James Norris. In 1972 she'd decided to undergo a sex change. Of all the Sunday Times team, it was Morris who was closest to Holden. They went back a long way, working together when they were roving between various publications; they "stood up to each other", Campbell was told, and they "had a special bond". So Campbell asked her about the postcard she'd received from Holden.

"True. We always used to send each other witty postcards wherever we travelled," agreed Morris. "Not the sort of cheap risqué type of wit you find in souvenir shops; the sort more directed at oneself. Self-deprecatory… you know… But the postcard I received from him, sent just hours before he died, as I now know, was dramatically different from any of the cards we'd sent over decades of friendship."

"How do you mean?"

"We always sent each other messages in comic rhymes or limerick form. Then suddenly this strange and serious message arrived. Judge for yourself…" Morris showed the postcard to Campbell. The sketch on the front was identical to the one on the card Holden sent to his wife, but this one had a chilling note on the reverse:

Pray for the peace of Jerusalem. Citadels still have their uses.

"Can you think of anything that can remotely explain the strange reference to the "citadels"? Is it possible it has a symbolic meaning? Maybe a private joke or anecdote?" asked Campbell, embarrassed.

"You mean a sexual connotation? I've been racking my brain, just thinking of anything I might have told him about the citadel of Jerusalem, or otherwise, but I can't think of anything, absolutely nothing!"

"Notice he used the plural, so he might be hinting at something that happened to you or him, perhaps in another citadel, and that event had been repeated for him in the citadel of Jerusalem, when he was there?" Morris paused but could not come up with any explanation.

"Look, I was an intelligence officer in the army in Palestine after the war… so of course the citadel of Jerusalem has an emotive significance. I might have talked to him about it. Also Jerusalem fell to the Romans in 70 AD after Jewish independence from the Holy Land, we're talking ancient history now, but I cannot for the life of me think of anything specific that occurred between myself and Dave that features any citadel, or any other citadel in the world." Morris could hardly have been more emphatic. "Do you know what disturbs me most about this? It's the seriousness of this postcard, knowing as I do now that he died a few hours after sending it. It's terrible. I'm worried that he may have done something silly, assuming he knew Palestinian wishes were not going to be taken into account at Mene House," said Morris with a tear in her eye.

"Are you saying that Holden might have been involved in activities outside his journalistic work?" Campbell sensed a breakthrough.

"Intelligence you mean? Listen honey… we, the war generation, were all involved in some sort of intelligence activities one way or another, but David? Nah, I doubt it. He was just a straightforward down-to-earth Geordie." Campbell, brought back down to earth herself, decided to finish the interview and asked Morris if she could keep the postcard, in case it became evidence later.

From an intelligence drought to an intelligence flood in a short space of time! Campbell had learnt so much about Holden and the complexity of the Palestinian and Israeli conflict. But how could she verify the accuracy or even the truth of any of the information given to her, when every single person she met could have some vested interest in steering her in a particular way? The politicians had their own short-term agendas and the journalists only wanted a scoop. Who could she trust? Campbell felt the only way she could proceed was by going back to basic investigative techniques: corroboration by others. She must check the witness accounts of ordinary people, the taxi drivers, the hotel receptionists, the travel agents, the barbers, and anyone who had no personal interest in hiding or directing the truth.

*

The plane carrying Holden's body arrived. The Egyptian investigator, Colonel Nabil Youssef, came out and introduced himself to Campbell, who registered the officer's barely disguised shock that the Sam greeting him was actually a woman. She didn't mind that, in fact she sort of enjoyed watching the shyness of any Egyptian man unfold. Later the two met with Chief Superintendent Raymond Snell at the Yard and Youssef briefed them both about the progress of the Egyptian investigation and told them everything he knew. Campbell felt Youssef was hiding some vital information, or hadn't caught onto something, but equally felt he was genuine and professional… and rather good looking: *maybe,* she thought, *he's acting dumb to make us do all the talking.* She and Youssef then went and joined the Sunday Times crowd for a meal at a Lebanese restaurant in Central London. Campbell kept deliberately quiet, just watching Youssef and the journalists interacting: some were trying out their knowledge of Arabic in front of him. She wanted to see if anyone would divulge any information, let slip some vital clues. She noted the micro-reaction on Youssef's face when Harold Evans asked him if he'd had a chance to speak to Mr. Morsi Sa'ad Al-Din. She could not have mistaken it. Nothing "dumb" about him. Youssef was definitely *hiding* something from her. Strange that Evans hadn't even mentioned that name to her when they spoke: she made a mental note of it.

She was also taken aback by the colonel's confident insistence that, without jurisdiction, as she reminded him, he should meet with the flight attendant, Nicki Webster, who had served Holden on his last flight. Campbell agreed reluctantly but on the condition that he would let her do the talking.

As they drove to meet Webster, Campbell enjoyed Youssef's mere presence, to the extent that she realised she was breathing him in. He was a stunning man, only slightly younger than her, and the car was feeling rather "charged". So it was a relief of sorts when they arrived at the Ramada Hotel near Heathrow, where the airline's cabin crew were stopping over on their flight from Washington to Amman.

"I must advise you Miss Webster that you are under no obligation to answer any questions, we are just gathering information about a British man murdered in Cairo on Tuesday December 6th. He arrived on a flight on which you were serving him." Campbell showed the flight attendant a recent photograph of Holden.

"Sure I will help you, of course… if I can," answered Webster quickly. After a few seconds she returned the photograph to Campbell. "I'm sorry, his face doesn't ring any bells." Her words came out quickly again and Campbell noticed that Webster wasn't engaging with the photograph, as though avoiding it.

"Look again, please, Miss Webster. More carefully this time…"

"We go through a lot of faces every day, Inspector, almost every face I see looks familiar somehow these days. It is difficult to say for sure, but I do remember this flight because it was the first time I served on the new Boeing 727. It is a much narrower model than usual, and so slightly harder work if you get what I mean... Okay... I do vaguely remember a British man, I think, who asked me which part of the north of England I was from. Yes, he was sitting next to this really talkative American lady, they weren't together, but then again... it's all just a fuzzy mess for me really... I might just as well be talking about a different man or a different flight altogether, so I'm sorry. My testimony's going to be completely useless..." She looked quickly back and forth at the two of them as she let out a slow breath.

"That's alright Miss Webster, it's not a problem at all." Campbell applied gentle pressure to Webster's hand to try to calm her down. "No testimony needed! We're just asking you if you might remember anything... anything at all... beyond what you've already told us." The DCI was also curious as to why Webster used the word "testimony", a word that didn't fit the context somehow. They thanked her and left. When back inside the car, Youssef announced that he had been summoned back to Egypt. He left shortly after, leaving Campbell to do the wondering alone.

*

The medical examiner who conducted the belated post-mortem on Holden's body inquest at London Hospital noted: *I agree with the Egyptian medical examiner regarding the cause of death being a single gunshot wound through the heart. There is bruising to the principal knuckle of the left middle finger, and to a lesser extent on fingers 3 and 4 of the same hand. There is discernible defensive fingertip bruising.* So Campbell knew the outcome of the inquest would be "unlawful killing abroad".

She was logging Holden's personal effects in the evidence room when, in the new spirit of sharing, she received a phone call from

Harold Evans. "Did you hear the news?" he said, then continued without waiting for Campbell to answer. "A Lebanese newspaper published an article saying that David was killed by the Egyptian Secret Service, mistaking him for another journalist, David Hudson, from the Guardian!"

Later, face-to-face again, Evans extrapolated the details of what he knew as fast as he could, worried about John Knight of the Daily Mirror breaking the news in the UK before he could. "Apparently the name Holden and Hudson are similar in Arabic script and they both have the same Christian name. The Egyptians had a bone to pick with Hudson and they got the surname mixed up with Holden." This puzzled Campbell. She really didn't think that the Egyptian government, on the verge of one of the biggest events in its modern history, would risk such a criminal act against a British journalist in their own capital, whether Holden or Hudson. The timing of the crime didn't fit. Unless the risk was worth taking for the Egyptians. This she could figure out by researching David Hudson, so she wasted no time in heading directly to The Guardian to meet with him, the paper's foreign correspondent. Evans set his printing presses to maximum speed, this time with Yard clearance.

Hudson told Campbell everything about his recent encounters with the Egyptian Secret Police. It all started with the "bread riots" earlier in the year, January 1977. The riots were popular and spontaneous, a big blow to Sadat's economic reforms and his "openness" to the West. Hudson had happened to be in Cairo and witnessed the riots himself. They rose up in many areas of Egypt but the eye of the storm was the industrial city of Helwan, a few miles south of the capital. The riots were triggered by Sadat's withdrawal of state subsidy on basic food stuffs resulting in higher prices. To make matters worse, the Egyptian police overreacted. Then Nabbawi became their minister. They could have let the situation burn itself out, which is what Nabbawi would have allowed had he taken his position earlier, but instead more than sixty people died in what turned into a conflict. Sadat was shaken by the scale of the riots, he'd thought he had a firm grip on Egypt and it was a rude wake-up call.

"People were hungry after Sadat's economic reforms," observed Hudson. "A new 'filthy rich' class soon emerged. Basic food prices rocketed beyond people's means and all they needed to revolt was some political touchpaper. Sadat was absent in Aswan with President Tito of Yugoslavia when it happened, so it took him a few days to rescind the inflammatory law, but the riots kept going and started to become violent. As if people were saying to themselves "since we started we might as well go all in and ask for more". Hudson smiled. "Reminds me of Macbeth… 'I am in blood stepped in so far, to go back would be as hard as to go o'er.' and like Macbeth's Scotland, the Arab world is ruled by the people's fear of the state. Once that fear barrier gets knocked a bit, anything can happen. Anyway, I went and wrote an article in The Guardian contrasting the nouveaux riches with the nouveaux pauvres and crossed a red line…" Campbell sat forward. "I criticised the First Lady, Mrs Jehanne Al-Sadat, and her luxury lifestyle, and boy did they hate me for that."

15

David Hudson told Campbell that the Egyptian authorities thought that the riots were the work of communist agitation and accused Hudson of distorting the truth about Egypt, before expelling him later in January. Hudson confided that he was practically assaulted at the hotel, a group of army officers stormed his room at the Cosmopolitan, made him pack his bags in front of them and then took him at gunpoint directly to the airport, putting him on the next flight to London. Afterwards, they called him all sorts of names. Musa Sabri, the editor of the Al-Akhbar newspaper, called Hudson a Jew. Apparently just because his first name was David. Hudson explained to her that he didn't in the least object to being called a Jew, even though he wasn't, but it was meant pejoratively.

"So what happened after?" asked Campbell.

"I went back of course! I mean back to Egypt!"

"What? Was that even on the table? They let you in again?"

"Not quite! When the Foreign Secretary David Owen, note the name, decided to visit Cairo in April of this year, I joined the British press contingent going with him. I knew my arrival would be a problem so I applied for an entry visa via the British Embassy in Rome. I knew the London Embassy wouldn't play ball! So all the press contingent, me included, flew in on the same plane as David Owen. On arrival in Cairo they checked our papers, spotted my name and refused me entry; asked me to stay on the plane. But The Times foreign correspondent at the time, Robert Fisk, threatened that the whole British press would pull out of the trip if they excluded me! The Egyptians reluctantly backed down and we stayed for just two days, made sure we covered Owen's visit only, and then we left for Saudi Arabia. They kept a close watch on me during those two days and I came to know that Sadat was incensed by my being granted a visa and blamed his Minister of Interior. The previous one."

"Do you think this is why he sacked him and gave his post to Nabbawi?" asked Campbell.

"Yeah, probably."

"Okay. So here's my big question to you, Mr. Hudson! Do you think it possible that the Egyptians got Holden's name mixed up with yours? Did they mean to kill you, and not Holden?"

"There are factors making this theory implausible somehow," said Hudson.

"Such as…?"

"Timing, for a start. Egypt was preparing itself for the biggest event in its modern history, the Israeli and American delegations were due to arrive in Cairo, and the UN… the whole world…was watching, literally. It was vital for them to show that the capital is secure and that they're in full control. How could they risk such an operation against a British journalist? Also, government agencies don't kill unless there is a tangible benefit for them. What tangible benefit would the Egyptians gain by eliminating me? None! There are still many other journalists who can continue writing about the regime in Egypt or the living conditions of the Egyptian people."

"Did you try to go again? I mean to cover the Peace Conference like Holden?" asked Campbell.

"No! That's why I think this theory is unlikely. The Guardian decided to send someone else and I was only asked to cover the Palestinian angle of Sadat's peace initiative, which is my area of interest."

"So, what's your take on the Holden case?" asked Campbell, hoping to glean ideas from a man who knew Egypt first-hand.

"I'm not sure ... Look I knew Holden for years – a decent fellow and a talented writer. Older than me, a different generation. We always considered him to be an establishment man... his contacts and sources tended to be the conservative types, even the Palestinian ones."

"Anyone in particular?" asked Campbell.

"Well, you can start here in London. Said Hammami is the PLO representative in London, an ambassador for the Palestinian people in the UK, a close associate of Yasser Arafat and a well-known moderate. Very pleasant chap actually, you should meet him. He got on well with Holden I believe, so he might give you more insights."

"Holden didn't just cover Palestine, right?" Campbell said.

"No. He had a wide and solid knowledge base for foreign affairs generally, but he did get one or two things wrong...one rather memorably so..."

"Like what?"

"Like denying the Americans were ever involved in the bloody 1973 coup d'état in Chile. That was very uncharacteristic of him everyone thought. Even the CIA had trouble denying their involvement in that terrible coup. That wouldn't have been so bad had he not written, before the event, that a coup was likely to take place in Chile. So when it did happen, people wondered whether Holden was more than a journalist; you know...was privy to information or..."

"Or...?"

"...or even playing a role."

"He might have been a spy?"

"I doubt it. Too solid and professional for that wouldn't you say? Journalists who become spies are normally pretty mediocre. Holden was not mediocre." He stubbed out a cigarette.

Campbell came out of her meeting with Hudson with one name ringing in her ears: Said Hammami. It was time! She needed a perspective into understanding Middle Eastern politics. And where better to start than with an understanding of the worst conflict to plague the region, the very conflict that Holden himself may have died for.

On Monday 2 January 1978, a bank holiday, and the day before two Syrian Embassy staff died in a mysterious car bomb in Mayfair, Campbell arranged to meet Hammami at Manzi's just off Leicester Square. The restaurant was run by an Italian family and was Hammami's favourite meeting place. Campbell was impressed by Hammami, a true gentleman and naturally attractive. He was soft spoken with good English, even though he hadn't studied in a Western university. He started talking to Campbell as if he had known her for years, talked about his two children non-stop; how academically gifted his daughter was for her age. Campbell warmed to Hammami instantly; she felt he was sincere and likeable, with no pretensions. He told her how shocked he was about Holden's killing but added that he was not surprised either. So Campbell asked him what he knew about Holden that made him express such a comment.

"Damascus, DCI Campbell, where all roads lead to," said Hammami. "It's pure speculation on my part, but if I was a betting man I'd wager that Holden was killed on the orders of Hafez Al-Assad. But first you have to bear with me as I explain a few things to you."

Campbell was happy to sit back in comfortable surroundings and listen to a quiet, measured voice. "Holden had a soft spot for people who were victimised by British post-colonial policies, like the Arabs and particularly the Palestinians. So naturally his views were somewhat against Israel. On the other hand, the Israelis sub-divide their Western critics: either they are antisemitic in the traditional Western sense or, if they are Jewish themselves, then they must be self-haters. It was black and white. But Holden was an anomaly for them, he didn't fit within their thinking. Holden was not antisemitic, far from it. So yes, the Israelis were probably relieved to hear he was killed, but did they kill him? I very much doubt it."

"Why?" asked Campbell, puzzled by this Palestinian who, for a change, did not accuse Israel of all the ills in the world.

"Well, I have to take you back a bit. It all started with the civil war now raging in Lebanon. At the beginning, Israel had wanted to remove the Palestinians from south Lebanon for many years, especially after the Entebbe hijacking in 76, so when civil war broke out it gave them an opportunity to achieve their aim. But the civil war in Lebanon was so dynamic for everyone that it was difficult keeping up with the shifting alliances. That summer, Hafiz Al-Assad of Syria intervened and occupied parts of Lebanon. This created a stand-off with Israel and Syria perfectly balanced, maintaining an in-limbo state… neither war nor peace. The two countries thrived and perpetuated that status quo, letting the Lebanese factions play it out among themselves. My boss, Yasser Arafat, stuck between the Israelis and the Christian Maronites, was faced with a difficult choice. If we lost Lebanon, Arafat was finished and the hard-line Rejectionists would take over, returning the area to the dark period of political assassinations and Black September. So when Sadat's peace initiative sprung up into the equation, all the Palestinian factions came to the conclusion that they should use this as an opportunity to achieve peace."

"What? … Even the Rejectionists?" asked Campbell.

"Especially the Rejectionists!" Hammami shot back.

"And this is relevant to Holden, how?"

"I will get to that, please be patient. For the first time all Palestinian factions agreed that their time in Lebanon was up and that the only option was to talk peace with Israel, through Sadat. But two important people were secretly reluctant about any peace in the region at this point; the Israeli Prime Minister Menachem Begin and Syrian

President Hafiz Al-Assad. The two men, supposed enemies, actually agreed on something, albeit for their own different reasons. Both wanted the stalemate to continue… and any Palestinian shift towards peace would upset the balance…"

"How can anyone be upset about peace?"

"Aha! This is where Holden comes in. Holden believed in a concept which is probably a hundred years ahead of its time… He didn't believe in the two-state solution, one for the Israelis and the other for Palestinians, he believed all this nationalism and communism sweeping across the Middle East was just a temporary phase and would soon disappear. He saw an opportunity in Israeli know-how and Palestinian muscle coming together into one state. He advocated the concept of one nation for all, where everyone would be equal. Holden was impressed by how much better-off the Israeli Arabs are compared to their brothers in the Palestinian diaspora."

Campbell recalled at that point Holden's 1946 "visionary" article, the one published in his father's newspaper. "So he wanted to get the Israeli moderates and the Palestinian moderates to talk to each other?"

"But Detective Chief Inspector," Hammami smiled, "the Israeli moderates and the Palestinian moderates have been talking to each other for decades! Holden wanted to get the extremists from both sides talking! It seems he had sounded this idea out to the Saudi leaders while he was working on his book about the House of Saud. The Saudis are keen to solve the Arab-Israeli conflict in order for the Jewish lobby in the US to allow the Saudis to invest in the US market. This is what Holden told me when I met him a few months ago. But what I am betting on is that Holden, when he went to Damascus, sounded out this idea to the Palestinian extremists and was surprised how amenable they were to Sadat's peace intiative." He stopped, as if flicking through everything he'd said and checking he'd not left anything out. Then he smiled warmly again. "Look, I'm going to Lebanon next week and can find out more if you wish. I believe that he later sounded the idea out with King Hussein as well – you know they were personal friends, right?" But he continued without waiting for a reaction from Campbell. "President Assad was incensed at this prospect. He needed the Palestinians to stay under his control, nothing more, nothing less. What is worse, the Israelis too didn't want any such talks, and I stake my life that this is why Holden was killed... by the Syrians. Holden didn't die because he was disrupting Sadat's peace initiative as some papers are saying, on the contrary, I bet he died because he wanted a lasting peace in Palestine, with Palestinians living under a democratic system as equal citizens with the Israelis in one state. And only the Syrians didn't want that to happen."

Campbell left the restaurant overwhelmed... overwhelmed by facts and gratitude in equal measure. What a catch! Hammami had given her a completely new perspective on Holden's thoughts; more than anyone she had met so far. And so generously and intelligently. Holden wasn't a spy but probably meddled in some politics, trying to act as an intermediary between two desperately warring factions hoping to solve one of the most complex and sustained conflicts in the world.

*

Two days after his meeting with Campbell, two gunmen entered Hammami's London office and assassinated him. On hearing of his murder, and how close she was to a warm trail, she went straight to The Times and back to Edward Mortimer's office. He saw her through the glass wall from afar, guessed what she was after, excused himself from his meeting, and came outside to meet her.

"It didn't take you long to think about my idea!"

"You were absolutely right, I want to do it! I want to go to Egypt disguised as a tourist or a journalist, but on condition that no one is to know about this except you, and you don't ask me about what I find there."

"And in return you keep my contact in Egypt a secret too. That's fine, leave it to me and I'll arrange everything for you. I'll contact you in a day or two after the New Year."

*

"Take this new murder case, Sam. It might well be connected with the Holden case, and you seem certain the gunmen were Syrian." Snell knew it made complete sense for his DCI to handle both murders. But to his surprise, Campbell was in no mood for this new assignment.

"No, guv, I respectively decline. The real perpetrators are not here in London, they are abroad. Give the case to the anti-terrorist squad and let them play with it. I'm taking two weeks' leave, with your permission of course."

"What! Why? Is everything alright at home?"

"Yes, guv, I just need a holiday, after a long time without one. I've decided on Egypt!"

16

Sam Campbell went alone. Her relationship with her husband, Stephen, was on the rocks; he was busy with his own work anyway. Christmas and New Year had passed without any real passion between them. She too needed time to think about her life away from him, to take stock, assess if she still loved him or whether she should start a new life altogether. On January 10th 1978, Campbell took the first direct flight from Heathrow to Cairo. She had never been there before, in fact she hadn't been anywhere abroad apart from France and that was years ago with her dad.

She also went without applying for an entry visa in London, believing she'd have a better chance of entering the country by applying on arrival, just like Holden did. Her undercover occupation would be that of a teacher coming to Egypt for tourism. Campbell spent the whole journey, the waiting time at the airport and the flight time, turning over the various facts and theories of Holden's murder. She didn't have a strong feeling about any of theories she'd heard, though she forged a sentimental attachment to her conversations with Hammami and Mortimer. But without evidence…? It was all useless. Now she'd be on the ground, paddling through the minutiae, treading on dangerous territories, literally. Her biggest worry was bumping into

Colonel Youssef, or somehow him getting to know about her coming to Cairo and blowing her cover. But that was a battle for another day.

She decided to retrace Holden's last steps herself, as much as possible. She chose to fly in just before midnight, on a Tuesday night, just as Holden had over a month ago. Campbell imagined people should mostly be the same if they were working in shifts, down to the passport control officers and taxi drivers. This was her theory. She experienced the same chaos at the airport. After a long queue at passport control, she filled in the visa application form, her occupation and the purpose of her visit as agreed with Mortimer. The officer (could it be the same one?) asked her, "Are you visiting Egypt alone? Or with a group?" Mortimer had told her exactly what to say.

"I will be staying at the Hilton Hotel but will be visiting an old friend of mine, she is living in Cairo." The officer seemed to accept this, got his fee for the visa, stamped her passport and let her in. Campbell walked down the ponderous terrazzo corridor to the baggage reclaim area slowly, trying to imagine what Holden might have seen. She saw the exchange bureau, where Holden collected his Egyptian currency. She changed some money herself and signed the generic declaration that she'd only use the local currency in Egypt. She took her bag and proceeded through "nothing-to-declare" to the foyer outside. She spotted through the glass the taxi rank area outside the airport. As she was scanning the foyer for clues, a European-looking woman of middle-age approached her.

"Mrs. Campbell? ... My name is Eileen Gibson, Edward Mortimer asked me to meet you here, welcome to Cairo."

Eileen Gibson was exactly what Campbell would have ordered! She was English for a start, and the same age. She spoke fluent Arabic with the Egyptian dialect. On the way from the airport to the hotel, Gibson told Campbell how sorry she was about Holden; that she'd collaborated with him on a few publications and their paths crossed a few times in the interests of assisting Palestinians to get a fair deal. They also spoke about the tragic assassination of Hammami, but Gibson doubted that the two murders were connected. "Holden was a good friend of many Palestinians from the whole spectrum, but he was wholeheartedly for peace. Unlikely to disrupt or influence Sadat's peace initiative. Hammami was definitely killed by extremists. Abu Nidal most likely. It's different when one of their own talks publicly about peace."

Campbell was not going to speculate, and certainly didn't share with Gibson her discussion with Hammami, two days before his murder, about the Syrians being behind Holden's murder. She'd come to Egypt to find evidence, maybe not the forensic type but at least circumstantial.

*

Campbell chose to stay in the Hilton in Cairo. This is what Holden believed he'd booked last, or rather what others believed. She arrived late at night and crashed into bed as soon as she was checked in. Only to be awoken from her hard-earned sleep at dawn by the melodious calls to prayer of the muezzins. The whole trip, the atmosphere of the airport and the people, was a new experience for Campbell. In the morning at breakfast, the waiter who served her spoke good English. He seemed decent; told her he was Sudanese; his name was Hassan. Campbell tested his clout by asking him to change her room to one with a view of the Nile. After a few minutes he came back with the assistant manager, and a new room key! Campbell tipped Hassan and then asked him for another favour. She told him she'd reward him if he could get her copies of the telexes from this hotel and from the Meridien, detailing how Holden's bookings were changed between November 27th to December 7th. She offered Hassan 50 Egyptian pounds; a substantial sum, and told him he would get the same amount again if he brought her a printout of these telexes. This was more than three months' salary for Hassan. After a couple of days he had handed her the printout, for both hotels! But Hassan told her that the police had been sniffing around him ever since he'd asked about these telexes. He'd had to pay off a few people including the police to ease the process. Campbell paid him extra, took the printout and headed to her room. She laid out all the telexes on her bed and the floor in chronological order. At last! The telexes that the Sunday Times couldn't give her!

On Friday 25 November 1977 two separate requests were sent by the Sunday Times in London asking about availability of a single room for one week starting Friday 2 December, one request to the Hilton Cairo and the same to the Meridien. The Hilton confirmed availability on that day but the Meridien was fully booked for that weekend. The Sunday Times then confirmed the two bookings, one at the Hilton for Friday 2 December for one week (as stated on Holden's airline ticket) and a second booking at the Meridien (Holden's preferred hotel) for Saturday 3 December after the weekend in Cairo. Campbell discovered that the Cairo weekend was Thursday and Friday. She also learnt that Holden preferred the Meridien because it was close to Mene House.

It was the busy season for hotels in Cairo in the run up to Christmas. The policy was that one could cancel up to 24 hours before arrival with no penalty. Campbell concluded that Holden, before he even left London, requested that both bookings be kept alive in case he changed the date of his arrival. This meant Holden did think about the possibility of delaying his arrival in Cairo and this fitted well with his last-minute decision to go the West Bank. He thought he had this option open from day one.

On Monday 28 November 1977, a day after Holden arrived in Damascus, a request was made from the Sunday Times in London to push the Hilton Cairo booking back by one day to Saturday 3 December, for the airline ticket to be altered, and for the Meridien Cairo booking to be cancelled altogether. So it was at this point that

Holden had fixed his Cairo arrival date. Not as she had thought.

Then no telexes were sent to Cairo until Friday 2 December 1977. When Holden was in Amman, a request came from the Sunday Times in London to cancel the Hilton booking and this time request of the Meridien Cairo a single room for one week, starting Monday 5 December. The Meridien confirmed availability but stated that the booking would only be open until Sunday 4 December and would be cancelled if no confirmation was received. Normal policy for most hotels in Cairo and Holden was likely aware of it. This fitted well with Holden's decision to go to the West Bank with Mortimer the next day. So he'd informed the Sunday Times of his change of plan, fixed the Meridien booking and cancelled the Hilton one.

But on Sunday 4 December, the day when Holden travelled from Amman to the West Bank, a request came from the Sunday Times in London to push the Meridien Cairo booking back by one day to Tuesday 6 December, and also book the Hilton Cairo for the same day. But surprisingly the Meridien rejected the booking. The Hilton confirmed the new booking which would be open until Monday 5 December and cancelled if no confirmation was received. Campbell learnt that on that same day, the Egyptian government requested the Meridien Hotel be reserved for journalists only due to its proximity to Mene House, and not to accept any new bookings unless they came approved by the Egyptian government.

On Tuesday 6 December, just hours before the murder, at 21:35 Cairo time, two requests came into the Meridien and Hilton, almost at the same time, to cancel the bookings for David Holden, even though the booking for the Meridien was not confirmed anyway. The telexes also quoted the correct reference numbers. But, this time, what was more surprising was that the two telexes did not come from the Sunday Times in London. They came from the Intercontinental Hotel in Amman where Holden was staying!

This was exactly the sort of clue Campbell was looking for. When those two telexes were sent, Holden would have been 30,000 feet in the air on his way to Cairo. Now she knew that someone in Amman had made sure that the two hotel bookings were cancelled so that neither hotel would raise any alarm over his non-arrival. No one would miss him. This, Campbell thought, fitted well with the acts of removing all identification from the body. She independently came to the same conclusion as Youssef had in Cairo: that it was not only important to know which booking was open, it was actually more important to know which booking Holden thought he had at the time of his arrival. Campbell was surprised that the Sunday Times journalists didn't know about this, and, more so, that neither did the Egyptian police. Or could they have known... and kept this information from her? She was determined to find out who at the Intercontinental Hotel in Amman had requested the sending of these telexes, and more importantly, on whose orders. But she also had to ask Gibson to connect her with a few more people. The first being the first person on the scene; not from the police, but the very first, a medical student, who found the body in the early hours of that morning.

Finally Campbell visited the site where Holden was dumped, it was a small desert area located in Madinet Nasr district. She could see that the area was situated between two unconnected neighbourhoods and that a new road had recently been built connecting the two. The road had unpaved verges on both sides and she could see that in a few years the area would have evolved to be fully developed. This was, said Gibson, how Cairo had developed over the decades: haphazardly and without forward planning. Towns grew organically, sometimes against all logic. The road along which Holden was found had no name. "Now they're already calling it the David Holden Road," Gibson told Campbell. The wasteland to the sides of it was covered with a pale soft dirt, softer than dune sand. Like cooking flour but beige in colour.

Holden must have been carried to the spot as there were found no traces of the powder on his shoes or clothes. Dust like that would have hid in the grooves of Holden's corduroy suit. It was clear that this was not the murder scene. Of course, Campbell knew this. But it was surprisingly worthwhile seeing it first-hand, and besides she was actually enjoying flexing her investigative muscles at last. Yes, she could now see that the murder scene was ideal for its proximity to the centre of Cairo, and the airport, but also in terms of its seclusion, especially at night.

Strangely, Campbell was in her element ever since she arrived in Cairo. She felt a sense of control, that she had been missing, in this investigation. Just one thing mitigated the DCI's enjoyment in her undercover search in Cairo, to the same degree that it added to it! She sensed always that she was being watched. Not necessarily by the same person. There was always someone in the hotel looking in her direction and bumping into her too many times. Chambermaids rummaging through her bag and clothes in the wardrobe; sometimes a car following her, a different one each day. "Don't worry about it for a second," said Gibson. "That's normal here. Egypt is a nation of informers. They watch all foreigners, especially if they're not part of a rowdy package holiday. It's a hangover from Nasser." Campbell was experiencing a new life. A door had opened. An Egyptian life.

17

It took Gibson's contacts in Egypt no time to trace Bilal Othman Ibrahim, the medical student who found Holden dead, and to arrange a meeting with him in a coffee shop deep in the Old City in Khan Al-Khalili, not far from the Al-Azhar Medical University. For Campbell, Ibrahim was an important witness, he was the first person to see Holden dead. He might tell her things missed in the police reports.

He was thin and tall and looked nervous, making an effort to speak basic English. He kept looking around him, though Gibson had chosen the time of the meeting to be at the height of the afternoon, when there would be fewer people. "Even informers have to have their siestas," she'd joked to Campbell.

Settled in a quiet area of the coffee shop, Gibson tried to calm Ibrahim to get him to open up to them. She played the human angle which always works in Egypt. She told him to fear nothing from them, that she and Campbell were relatives of Holden, the 'English one', and were simply trying to establish what had happened to him. After a while, and with the perennial glass of tea and small talk, Ibrahim started to relax a little and open up. "I cannot forget the face of the English one," Ibrahim said to them. "Like he is laughing but little." He tried to imitate Holden's smile himself, something that could have proved traumatic or at least insensitive to genuine relatives of the deceased. Campbell knew all of this since she had seen the body herself and she too found it difficult to explain the smile on Holden's face. It was akin to a smirk that looked somewhat arrogant; a smile that had an element of contempt in it. Aimed where? At his assassins? At the whole duplicitous world?

They went over the time when Ibrahim spotted the body, where exactly he was, the reasons he was using this desert road and all the questions that the police asked, temporarily forgetting their cover story. They felt that poor Ibrahim knew his answers by heart, as if he had memorized what he'd said to the Egyptian police. But Campbell did spot some irregularities in Ibrahim's answers. He claimed he was on his way to the mosque for the Fajr prayer at dawn. Campbell, a light sleeper, knew that dawn was at 5.28am when she arrived in Cairo but allowing for the daily changes in the movement of the sun over the year, dawn would have been at 5.15am on Wednesday 7 December, the day of Holden's murder. Normally, though dawn, it would have remained pitch dark for almost 45 minutes after that time until enough daylight had broken to make surroundings visible enough for discoveries. Yet Ibrahim told them there was enough light for him to be able to "see" the body. Also, if this is the case, why did Ibrahim only report the body to the police at 7am?

Anomaly number two, Youssef had told her that Holden was spotted by a student at 8.30am. She felt that Ibrahim was giving more information than someone who just discovered a body by chance. Campbell gave Ibrahim a hard time questioning these anomalies, and he became agitated. Gibson tried to soften the tone, but the more agitated he became the more he let out new information, and the more contradictions he offered them. Campbell was worried that he might leave them and withdraw from helping them, so she eased off. Gibson, taking the hint, changed the subject and asked him about general stuff, about his life, his family and his studies. Before long they had started talking about politics and current affairs, about the riots, the communists and conservative Islamists. He warmed to Gibson more than to Campbell, started to relax and talk, one subject leading to another as he talked about TV programmes and movies. Gibson told Ibrahim how much freedom the British had compared to the Egyptians: "We English viewers can even ridicule the Queen's Christmas Speech if we want…" Gibson said to him, something unimaginable to a citizen under Egyptian rule.

Ibrahim then laughed and let slip in broken English, "If you do this in Egypt they will put you on the road like Mr. Holden."

Campbell pounced. "What do you mean by 'put', Ibrahim? Do you mean Holden was 'put' there?" Ibrahim started to stammer, hesitated, said that he meant "kill" not "put". Then he said that he knew from the newspapers that he was put there by his killers. Campbell was unconvinced. The discussion didn't make sense to her, so she kept on with her probing of Ibrahim but this time she brought a personal dimension to their talk, a technique she'd employed with many witnesses before. Witnesses who she judged to be innocent but who didn't want to divulge essential information, most likely for fear of being drawn into something that frightened them. She told him her cover story that her sister Ruth, Holden's wife, needed answers to this mad murder and that the Egyptian police were not telling her anything at all. So if Ibrahim was hiding anything he should not fear retribution from her. Ibrahim, for his part, knew that he had divulged more than he should have, and had made himself vulnerable. He started begging them to promise they would not tell anyone. They agreed and meant it too.

Using Gibson as a translator now that more information was expected, Ibrahim then told them that he had actually been on his way to the mosque to pray, and that he was early to catch the dawn prayer. He used that route, even though it wasn't the quickest, to avoid the police patrols that were always on the lookout for religious students, fearful of them joining religious opposition movements. On that Wednesday he had wanted to go even earlier as he made a nithir, a vow to God, to call the prayer in a nearby mosque, and had agreed beforehand with the Imam to do so. Ibrahim's father had been through a difficult stomach operation and was in a critical condition. He'd made a pledge with Allah and promised that if his father survived the operation then he would call the prayer from a mosque in return. On his way, around 5am, as dark as night-time, the moon was hardly visible on that night, he saw a dark colour Fiat Nasr car pull over to the side of the road quietly. Ibrahim spotted the car from a distance, he hid from the view of the driver crouched behind a large dumpster by the edge of the road. There was a lamppost around ten metres from him but it was a little dim. Enough to light a small area of paving. He noticed the approaching car did not have its headlights on, and he didn't like that either. He thought they might be police. He decided to hide for a little, anticipating that the car would soon move on. But instead, he watched the car pull over and stop by the dumpster where he was crouched. Ibrahim froze; he didn't know what to do. Get out and show himself to them? He figured they were most likely drunks or druggies stopping to urinate, so he continued his wait.

It was what happened afterwards that made Ibrahim fear for his life. He saw two people exit the car, one from the front passenger seat and the second from the back. The two came out and lifted a third man who looked to be sleeping. The driver stayed in the car. Ibrahim had a good view of the driver from his hiding position, there was reasonable moonlight at the time, not a full moon but bright enough for Ibrahim to have a good look at the profile of the driver's face. He noticed a scar running diagonally across his cheek. But Ibrahim didn't see much else, other than how fast they dumped the third man. "Like it was practiced many times together," said Ibrahim. Still playing the concerned sister-in-law, Campbell asked Ibrahim what the men looked and sounded like. Ibrahim said that they looked Egyptian to him, or certainly Arab, wearing unremarkable clothes and that they didn't utter a single word for him to know where they were from.

He said he felt relieved when the car pulled away. He guessed they were some drunk losers dropping their intoxicated mate on the road and leaving him there to sober up. These things happened frequently in Cairo late at night or in the early hours… people meet a random guy and get drunk with him and when he is too drunk to tell them where he lives they drop him anywhere to let him sleep it off. But Ibrahim felt that it was too cold for such behaviour on that night and that the man would definitely freeze to death if he was left unattended. So, when he was sure that no one was around, Ibrahim came out from behind the dumpster and walked slowly and quietly towards the man. It was still dark.

As Ibrahim approached the man he was struck by the way he was left there; neat and tidy. The man himself was neat and tidy too. He was laid "like a vampire, like in the films" and Ibrahim showed them the positioning of Holden's two crossed hands. Campbell knew that was accurate.

"So did you tell the police all that? You should have … there's nothing wrong in what you've said to us so far… nothing to make you worry."

"Yes, and this is what I thought too. I did call the police, until…" Ibrahim switched back to speaking in Arabic. "You see first I called out to Mr. Holden. Trying to wake him up. I have come across many drunks like that in the past, sleeping on the street, but you can normally hear them breath loudly, like snoring, or they even respond when you talk to them. A sound or a whine, something, you can at least tell they are alive that way. But this man was not responsive. I thought he may have already frozen to death and his mates had just wanted to be rid of him out of self-preservation. By then though, some daylight was starting to break through the dark, and a few cars started to pass by too. Some drivers definitely saw me standing at that spot, but no one stopped." Ibrahim added that when he realised that the man was dead and that he looked like a Khawaja, Egyptian for foreigner, he had to contact the police and tell them everything, otherwise someone might have witnessed him standing by that spot and suspect him. So Ibrahim walked around the university campus to a newspaper kiosk known to have a public telephone, and he contacted the police. "There is a body of a Khawaja left by the road!" Ibrahim then told them how much he regretted his choice of words. They asked him to explain what he meant.

18

Bilal Ibrahim continued. He told the two women, who he now trusted completely, that when he rang the police and told them about Holden the operator had told him to wait by the body, to not allow anyone to come near him and to not talk to anyone. It took the police around 25 minutes to arrive at the scene, which Gibson interjected was fast for that area; and all that time only a few cars passed by and even fewer pedestrians. A couple of people stopped and asked Ibrahim about the "story of the lying man" but left quickly when he told them he was waiting for the police.

A large police car pulled over and two uniformed police officers got out. Ibrahim was standing by the body at first. But they waved to him to move as though to say don't talk to us yet and Ibrahim moved back. In fact they ignored him completely and went straight over to Holden's body, examining it from close up. They too might have thought he was sleeping off too much alcohol. One of the policemen crouched over the body and tried to wake Holden up. The other remained standing, as if on alert. Ibrahim moved across from his spot so that he was facing them, reminding them without speaking that he was still there, waiting for his turn to talk and tell them everything he knew. But when he looked at the officer crouching in the generous rising sun rays over the dead David Holden…"I almost died in my skin". He waited dramatically, for them to ask him why. His hushed gravity matched the import of his words: "the policeman who knelt by Mr. Holden's corpse had the same diagonal scar as the driver of the car had an hour earlier."

His audience, for it had suddenly turned into a theatrical production, felt their skin prickle. *Surely,* thought Campbell, *this can't be true.* She suspected he might be making it up to engage them, two impressionable, grieving English ladies. But she had only to look again at the genuine fear etched across the medical student's face to know that he was deadly serious.

"Ibrahim… Let's be clear… Are you saying that the driver of the green car whom you saw wearing plain clothes, was actually the same uniformed Egyptian police officer who came to the scene later?"

"I am sure of it, but I cannot say the colour of the car for sure because it was dark everywhere. It was not white, it was a darker colour," said Ibrahim in English. He then asked them not to contact him again and exited the stage that the unsuspecting coffee shop had provided.

*

The afternoon was waning. It was early evening when Ibrahim left the two women. Suddenly, tourists filled the coffee shop and all the narrow alleyways around them. Campbell and Gibson were stunned, reeling from what they had learnt from Ibrahim. *Holden… killed by the Egyptian police?* What were they to make of that? And what were the implications for their own safety? Gibson certainly hadn't expected a dangerous collision path with the Egyptian authorities. Now they had to be extra careful, must stick to their cover stories. With that in mind, the two women had to rush to their appointment with Imad Jawhar, the Reuters journalist who had identified the body at the morgue.

Jawhar was a friend of Holden and had been expecting his arrival, which was Campbell's main reason for wanting to meet him. He happened to know Gibson well through work, so he knew he was talking to a fellow journalist. But Gibson asked him to talk to "Ruth's sister" who was keen to know what had happened to Holden. He'd already told them that Holden had changed his itinerary back and forth several times and explained that he came to know the exact date and time of Holden's arrival from the main office of the New York Times. Campbell asked him to elaborate on how he had known of Holden's original schedule.

"Ah, okay. You see the New York Times Magazine in the US sent a request through our offices to interview President Sadat a week before Holden left London. They wanted Holden to do it for them and told our office here, requesting that we meet up with Holden on the assumption that the interview would go ahead. The interview was being arranged through Ashraf Marwan from the President's Information Office." Campbell had no idea who Ashraf Marwan was but let him continue, like a referee playing the advantage. "But Holden was keen to meet Ismail Fahmi, the Deputy Prime Minister who'd resigned after Sadat visited Jerusalem. Everyone thought that he resigned in protest against the peace initiative with Israel. Holden knew Fahmi as a friend and he gave our office the impression that he was more keen on meeting him than he was on meeting Sadat! So we arranged the Fahmi interview for Sunday December 4th at his residence in Ma'adi. Holden was preparing for it." Jawhar then said, "All this was arranged when Holden was still in London." When Gibson asked why Holden was more interested to meet Fahmi, Jawhar said, "I think Holden was trying to gauge the strength of the Egyptian opposition to Sadat's peace initiative, before meeting with the President. A dangerous thing to do in this part of the world, as you know."

Campbell and Gibson did not let on to Jawhar about Hudson's theory, they just kept quiet and let him continue, until Campbell asked, "Did you tell the Egyptian police about the Fahmi interview?"

"No, I don't think so, but I expect they knew about it somehow. The Sunday Times definitely knew. Although all this became unimportant since the Fahmi interview was cancelled anyway… we thought that Holden had changed his mind about it and decided to go to Jerusalem for a couple of days instead, so it all became an irrelevant detail in the timeline of his murder… given that he was killed two days after that date."

"How did you know about the cancellation of Fahmi's interview?" asked Gibson.

"Our Reuters office in Tripoli, Libya, sent a telex to our Cairo office here on Sunday saying that Holden could not attend Fahmi's interview. Like I said, we thought at that time he'd decided to go to Tripoli where the rejectionist Arab States were holding a summit meeting, we thought he was in Tripoli when the telex came, but later we learnt that he actually went to Jerusalem instead…"

"Wait! Are you saying you received a telex and thought it was from Holden in Tripoli on Sunday December 4th?"

"Not quite, no. The telex we got was written in the third person saying something like 'Holden cannot make the interview scheduled today, please send apologies.' We knew it referred to the Fahmi interview."

Campbell was now more confused. She could quite accept within herself that an unknown person sending a telex on behalf of Holden from Tripoli days before his murder may not be important, but in the context of another unknown person sending a telex from Amman cancelling Holden's hotel bookings when he was on his way to Cairo, it became relevant, almost a pattern. Why would Holden choose such an odd way to inform Jawhar about not being able to attend the ex-deputy's interview? It didn't fit well into the existing various narratives.

"Is there a way to find out who sent the telex in Tripoli?" she asked.

"Pffff, you can try, but we already tried ourselves. It was chaos in Tripoli then."

"Why didn't you tell the Sunday Times about all this?"

"I did! They know! But it all turned out to be unimportant detail since the murder happened afterwards. We didn't think much more of it; journalists were always changing their plans as the events were unravelling around them. At one point we didn't know which event we should cover."

Campbell didn't know what to think of all this. Could there be someone on the Sunday Times also covering Holden's tracks? In London? Could the Holden case have a much more complex motive than she anticipated? Thoughts started to race in her head. So far she had resisted falling headlong into one of the many wild conspiracy theories, propagated by the daily papers. Holden a spy or a double agent even... she didn't believe any of that. But what Jawhar told them threw in some doubt. Someone in London might be hiding telexes from the staff and Campbell made a note to investigate this when she was back in London.

On her way back to her hotel she asked Gibson to come to her room to have a quick drink on the balcony overlooking the Nile, a good setting for reflecting on what they had learnt. Cairo, Gibson told her, usually looks beautiful at night, especially during the winter months. She accepted and it was good that she did. As they entered the room, they were greeted by writing in large letters on the dressing table mirror. Campbell's lipstick had been used for the letters and was left discarded on the floor.

The message read:

WE KNOW WHO YOU ARE,
AND WHY YOU ARE HERE.
GO HOME!

Campbell was concerned, but Gibson was scared. Campbell looked through her belongings but could see nothing taken or disturbed, apart from the lipstick. It seemed that whoever had been inside her room was there for one reason – to warn Campbell. She knew then that her cover had been blown.

They both sat thinking about who it might be. Gibson was worried it was the Egyptians; that they had probably watched them talking to the medical student Bilal Ibrahim, but Campbell didn't think so. She thought that if it was the Egyptians they wouldn't waste time writing a message like this. Rather she thought this the work of some foreign agency operating in Cairo that wasn't comfortable about her work on Holden. Gibson was worried about Campbell's safety after receiving such a threat.

"But Eileen, it's okay, there's no threat in this message. Look at it, all it says is that they know who I am and why I am here, advising me to go back home. It could be a friendly warning, might even be MI6."

"Or it could be the killers! These sorts of messages don't come from terrorists, I agree. Yes, this is more like foreign agency work, as you say. But nonetheless, Sam, we need to be careful now... and YOU need to be very careful." The two agreed that they needed to leave Cairo quickly. Campbell wanted to visit Amman anyway, to investigate the story behind the cancellation telexes. Gibson was concerned about her own safety too, so she asked if she could join Campbell. Bags were packed and the first plane to Amman was booked. They spent that evening in Cairo trying to relax their nerves after the longest of days, becoming closer as a result.

The next day, first thing, quietly and discreetly, Campbell checked out and waited on the street. Gibson pulled up in the back seat of a Volkswagen Beetle and waved at her to join her, the car taking them both to the airport. Campbell jumped in the front. She already had a ticket to Amman and only needed to switch the date, but Gibson had to buy a new ticket at the airport which took longer. All this wait tested their nerves as they feared they could be picked up by the Egyptian police at any time. Leaving Egypt through passport control was straightforward. Their flight was a Royal Jordanian flight but this time it was a Boeing 747 model, the one with a wide body, different from the one Holden took. Campbell asked an air steward to contact his airline in Amman. She wanted to meet Nicki Webster again, in Amman this time. She felt that Webster was definitely hiding something. Maybe if she met with her again, without Youssef being present, Nicki would open up.

19

Campbell and Gibson finally arrived in Jordan just before dusk. They were struck by the piercing cold of the desert weather, colder than in Cairo. They hadn't prepared for that! Campbell had begun to enjoy Gibson's company to the extent that she now considered her a good friend and confidante. She was impressed with Gibson's encyclopaedic knowledge of the Middle East and of every conflict its annals of history contained. Gibson was one of those eccentric Englishwomen who can never live in England; who may yearn to get back to it, visit it occasionally, but never live in it. "I think I will die here, in this part of the world," she told Campbell. "As soon as I arrive in Britain I feel my senses dulling." She was a new source of inspiration for Campbell, whose life was stuck in a rut, headed, it seemed, for separation. If not this year, then perhaps the next.

When they reached Amman, Campbell suggested they stay at the Intercontinental Hotel "… to trace Holden's last steps." When they arrived at the hotel, while the receptionist was busy searching, Campbell asked if she could have room 701. "It was recommended by a friend," she said. The receptionist looked puzzled, knowing for a fact that there was nothing special about the room or the view from the window, but he humoured her.

"Yes, it looks like I can offer you Room 701, madam." He continued. "It's a double room by the way, it can fit two persons, shall I book just the one room?"

"That would be fine," answered Campbell quickly and looked at Gibson who seemed rather astonished but she too exhausted to argue.

Astonishment turned into awkwardness as they both stood there looking at the large bed in the middle of the room. "I wanted to see if there are any clues left by Holden in this room, also get a feel for what he saw and experienced… even the view from the window may give us a clue," Campbell explained to Gibson. "This is the room Holden shared with Kinza Murid until the early hours, just before his departure to the West Bank."

Having rested a little, Gibson decided to take a shower while Campbell headed to the hotel lobby alone, to see if she could find anyone who could give her access to the telex room of the hotel. She pretended she was waiting to rendez-vous with someone in the lobby, just hanging and looking around. There was a travel agent in the lobby, Bisharah Travel Agency. She went inside and pretended to be enquiring about day excursions to the ancient city of Petra. It was the manager she was speaking to and it didn't take her long to strike up a rapport with him. She told him she was a journalist with the Sunday Times, it was easier that way she decided. The manager, whose name was Adib Khalid, said to her immediately "…but I shared everything I know about Holden with your colleagues, Mr. Paul and another man. All I saw was Holden in the lobby around lunchtime, going into the coffee shop with an old American couple. This was on Tuesday 6 December just before he left for the airport." Campbell asked him whether Holden had tried to change any of his bookings, made any enquiries about his trip, or perhaps asked any questions about his hotel booking in Cairo. Khalid answered that he recalled nothing else. She came close at that point to asking Khalid about the cancellation telex but something made her stop. She felt Khalid was telling her half-truths, which meant he wasn't to be trusted. He was too keen to emphasise that Holden arrived in the hotel in good time around lunchtime on that Tuesday; and that he was not rushing to catch his plane. So Campbell decided to tread carefully. Gibson had warned her that Mossad's strongest operation outside Israel was in Jordan, not the West Bank or Beirut as many think.

Campbell also knew that the "old American couple" Khalid had mentioned to her, were the husband-and-wife writers and archaeologists John and Isobel Fistere. They wrote many books jointly about the Holy Land, but one book in particular, according to Gibson, was an interesting one, published in the early 1960s and called *Jordan, the Holy Land.* The Fisteres were friends of King Hussein too; John used to write some of his speeches, so in return the King had written the foreword for that book. Gibson said it was a trap set for the King. That the Zionist hardliners used that book as new evidence to their "historical" claim that even Jordan, not only the West Bank, was part of Greater Israel, the Holy Land, and part therefore of the 1927 Balfour Declaration in which the British had promised them a national home in Palestine.

Harold Evans had told her in London that the Fisteres asserted that they only met Holden briefly in the hotel lobby in Amman and that he'd looked hassled, in a rush to go, worried that he might have lost his hotel booking in Cairo. They'd wished him good luck with his travels and left.

Campbell decided to go back to the room rather than attract any more attention on her first day. But she had noted the contradiction between the two versions of Holden's state of mind on that day, his last day. She still had to find her access to the hotel's telex room and contact Royal Jordanian Airlines about meeting up with Nicki Webster again. She went back into her room at the exact moment Gibson was getting out of the shower, dripping wet and wrapped in towels. Gibson apologised, embarrassed, but something deep in Campbell was aroused; she felt physically attracted to her.

Campbell had been married for many years and never questioned her sexuality; despite her rebellious nature she always conformed, in the end, to what English society expected of her. She'd gone out with boys from an early age, but always ended up doing boys' stuff with them! She'd naturally suppressed her feminine side, or rather been hardly aware of it. It was true that her marriage was coming to an end, but she had genuinely never imagined she'd see another woman as sexually attractive.

Gibson on the other hand was proud of her femininity and passionate about it, never ashamed to show it. But she had dedicated her life to the Middle Eastern struggle rather too much, perhaps to compensate for her unexplored sexuality. But hey, it was the 1970s after all. Life was different now and these two English women happened, genuinely unintentionally, to be in a hotel room together in the Middle East.

It wasn't clear who made the first move. Perhaps Gibson's towel had slipped a little with absolutely no encouragement from the wearer. Perhaps Campbell's visible fixation on what she could see of her friend's body – she particularly remembered the wet collar bone and the sweep of her thighs as they extended upwards, still wet, into the white hotel towel – propelled her intuitively into those beautiful, glistening, eccentric English arms. For Campbell it was the most enjoyable and spontaneous sex of her life and totally, utterly liberating. To be with a woman intensified her natural needs: they were both from Venus. There was no journeying into the 'other', no space for misunderstanding, and a knowledge that what felt great for her felt great for Gibson too: a hand pressed so hard against her breast that an entirely new route to the fire in her sex, pulsing down through the front of her upper body, was opened up; fingers that knew where to find the right spot, as though exploring a mirror image that needed to be made real. Gibson felt a huge relief too, hardly believing she'd just had sex with an English policewoman. And been so good at it! The plain fact was, the two of them were just attracted to each other in every way. After a sleepless but entirely refreshing all-nighter of talk and sex, cigarettes, more sex and then talk again, the two entered the morning hours feeling, okay, yes, a little embarrassed in the plain light of day, but more than anything, they felt right with the world. But Campbell had to repackage her feelings regarding her husband, not to mention the Egyptian colonel; with the tiptoeing that followed, Gibson picked up the signal that she would have to wait before there was a 'next time'.

Now they set out to find out who was telling the truth about Holden's behaviour at the hotel: Adib Khalid or the Fisteres. Campbell had quickly become an expert on how the Middle East worked: the information from the people who were working at the edges of the picture that the bigger players were painting was normally the most accurate and most helpful, the most revealing too. They did indeed help frame things more clearly, and Campbell loved a big picture. And who was more peripheral to a hotel than its bellboys? So Campbell, with Gibson's help, found a young man who was working as a bellboy at the hotel on that day. Adnan agreed to meet with them after his shift was finished.

A Palestinian from the village of Jalud in the West Bank, Bashar Adnan had come to Amman with his family after the 1967 Six-Days War. They all lived in the "Mukhayyim" or "tent camp" in Amman with other Palestinians evicted during the war. His father was a taxi driver working mostly from the hotel. Campbell then showed him a photograph of Holden and asked him if he'd seen him. "Yes, I remember him, he was the journalist who was killed, after leaving the hotel here, yes?" They nodded. "I told them many times, this man, left his bags in our left luggage, they were two items, a large red suitcase and a brown leather holdall, he took with him a small handbag, said he will be back in two days to pick them up, I remember because the large bag was heavy and it is our job to have good memories about people faces and their luggage, these are *amanah*." Gibson explained to Campbell that amanah meant "safe keeping until returned to the rightful owner" which was an important rule in their culture. "You see, after two days, this dead man, arrived at the hotel around 1.30 in afternoon, after he came back from the Palestine, and he asked me about his luggage, which were kept safe in our storeroom, so I took him to the storeroom. He opened his large red suitcase and also opened the small bag which he took with him to Palestine and then took one file, like a folder of papers, from the small bag he brought with him, and moved it to the large one which was left in Amman all the time, and then closed both of them quickly, and left all of his bags in the store room again. I could see what he was doing even standing at the end of the storeroom waiting," said Adnan. "He then gave me a good tip and asked me to call him a taxi, which was strange, I thought, since he just arrived by a taxi himself." Campbell guessed the folder of papers Holden brought with him from the West Bank in the red suitcase had been the petition, the one given to Holden by the Palestinian mayors in the West Bank for President Sadat. She then asked Adnan if he remembered which taxi driver took Holden, and where to.

"He didn't take the taxi in the end, Adib Khalid the travel agent in the lobby suddenly came out and offered Holden a lift, and he went with Khalid, you can ask him." Adnan looked for a reaction. "Then the dead man came back a couple of hours afterwards, in the evening, he was rushed and looking hassled, worried about his hotel booking in Cairo, but was delayed by the old American couple who talked to him for few minutes standing in the lobby." So the Fisteres had been right. Campbell was concerned. Khalid had said nothing about giving Holden a lift in his car. Gibson waved at Campbell to back off, hinting that they should now be careful as Khalid seemed most likely to be connected somehow to Holden's murder. They paid Adnan some money and asked him not to tell anyone about their meeting.

20

"I am sorry ladies, I cannot give you more information. Miss Webster left our airline." Mrs. Samia Radwan, the manager at the Royal Jordanian Airline in Amman looked genuinely disappointed not to be able to help.

"You mean she resigned? When did she resign, Mrs. Radwan?" asked Campbell.

"Not quite. Just after the New Year, she left in a hurry. If you see her, please tell her to pick up her cheque for the rest of her money… we owe her more than a month's salary!"

It turned out that Webster had resigned from her job after meeting with Campbell and Colonel Youssef in London. Campbell didn't even have to suspect any more, she was certain that the flight attendant left because of something to do with Holden's case. She'd been right to sense she was hiding something. But in confidence, Radwan showed the two women a copy of the flight manifest for RJ503 which they'd requested. The list of names contained the correct spelling of Holden's name, but with an impressive degree of foresight, Gibson asked Radwan if they could see the actual papers that were sent over to Egypt, not the airline transcript. The actual facsimile copy. After some wait, this is what Radwan gave them:

	English version	Arabic version
Airline computer system	David Holden	ديفيد هولدن
Actual facsimile	David Holden	ديفيد هيدسون

Campbell was disappointed, but Gibson read Arabic perfectly well and saw clearly that someone had translated Holden's name on the Arabic version as David Hudson. To the Arabs, the two names not only sound similar but also have similar shapes when both names are written in the Arabic alphabet. So someone in Amman, maybe deliberately, rendered Holden as Hudson as no one checked either language if the names matched. It was a clever trick. The obvious conclusion to be drawn, felt Campbell, was that someone wanted to trick the Egyptians into thinking that Holden was a much more hated journalist.

Finally, the seemingly interminable jigsaw was starting to reveal a clear picture. All that was needed was another piece to finish the puzzle: the telex requesting the cancellation of the hotel bookings. So they went back to the hotel, preparing to head back to London with a clear and convincing conclusion to the case.

Back in the hotel, Campbell elicited the final jigsaw piece from the manager. "I am not supposed to tell you this, madam, but the two telexes were sent at the request of the taxi driver Sulieman Rabi. He came to the desk after dropping Holden at the airport and told us that Mr. Holden had asked him to do so."

Campbell felt that she had stumbled into a minefield and that the clues had all been here in Amman, not in Cairo, and possibly not even in Jerusalem. Adnan the bellboy was tasked with finding out when Suleiman Rabi was likely to be back from the West Bank so they could speak to him next. In the meantime, they headed across the foyer to Adib Khalid, to confront him about his half-truths.

"I cannot tell you here, ladies, please meet me in a half hour at the coffee shop down the road," Khalid stammered. Accordingly, Campbell and Gibson went directly to the coffee shop and waited for almost an hour for Khalid to arrive, worrying the whole time that they might be treading too close for some to solving the Holden murder.

When Khalid showed up, he looked disturbed and sat down quickly and told them his story without any introduction. "When I offered Holden a lift he asked me to take him to the Royal Hashemite Court to meet someone there at the security gate and I left him there and went back. Initially I didn't even think about it, but after he was murdered I was worried I might get dragged into something bigger and wanted to be out of it. He did get back early evening, and he was in a rush to go to the airport to catch his flight when he met the old American couple. Please don't tell anyone that I talked to you, and please don't approach me again, I have a young family and want to get on with my life."

Khalid left the coffee shop and they followed a few yards behind him, on their way back to the hotel. Both trying to work out why Holden would be so keen to meet someone in the Royal Hashemite Court, so close to his final flight to Cairo. And why did the taxi driver Rabi tell the hotel to cancel Holden's hotel bookings after he'd dropped him at the airport? Above all, were the Egyptians even aware of the cancellation telexes? These were the new questions that needed urgent answering.

But as they walked on the narrow footway with no one around, except for Khalid walking ahead of them, a large American car pulled over right next to them with three local-looking men inside. Two men got out which made Campbell nervous but they seemed only to be asking Gibson for directions in Arabic. Gibson was starting to explain that they were not Amman locals when both women were pushed violently into the back of the car where guns were pressed against them. Quiet, the cold of the pistols told them, or be killed. Campbell and

Gibson had no option but to comply.

The car was driven flat out, taking a turn into a deserted road before stopping in wasteland. Campbell was blindfolded and dragged away from Gibson into another car... she later said it felt like a van because she was forced down onto what felt like a metal floor. The van was driven fast for around 40 minutes. Fully blindfolded and not hearing anyone talking, tossed around by the moving vehicle, Campbell knew there was just one man sitting next to her holding her hands tightly against a metal surface.

The van finally stopped, she heard the door open and again she was being dragged across rough ground. She almost tripped against the stones on the ground as she kept up with the man pulling her hard. She was scared, very scared. Now was not the time to be heroic, now was the time to be pragmatic and get out of this situation alive. It is all about self-preservation. The abductors stopped, held her firm, and finally lifted her blindfold. It took her eyes a few precious seconds to adjust to the glare of the Jordanian sun. As though they deliberately wanted the sun to be in her eyes, it hung there facing her with all its force. In front of her stood a blond European-looking man. He spoke English fluently, but with an accent, could have been Dutch, or Eastern European. He had the air of a boss.

"We asked you to go home DCI Campbell, not come to Jordan," he said to her.

"Who are you? Someone at the hotel will be raising the alarm with the British Embassy if I don't return safely... with my friend." Campbell adopted a forceful tone but her voice sounded hollow to her own ears, not belonging to her. The fact that this man looked European gave her some hope that she might escape with her life.

"Yes of course, your British embassy and your Palestinian-loving friend, we know. Don't worry, she'll be safe, we are used to people like Eileen Gibson. But tell me, what did the British embassy do for David Holden? Even after he died?" Campbell wanted to answer with something placatory but was puzzled.

"You killed him?" she asked, playing a hard card.

"Us? No! The Egyptians killed him, not us," the man said, as though it was common knowledge and not a revelation that so many, even then, were hoping to discover.

"But you tricked the Egyptians into thinking that Holden was actually Hudson, didn't you? Which makes you the real murderer. The Egyptians were fooled, so don't play the innocent with me," said Campbell, like an affronted parent. This case had got under her skin.

"If you want to see England again, stay out of it, DCI Campbell. This is bigger than you. The Egyptians wanted to murder a particular British man, we just directed them to a different one. Holden or Hudson, what does it matter for you? The result is still a British man killed by the Egyptians."

"Why kill Holden rather than Hudson?" asked Campbell, sensing her captor's need to share.

"Ah. In July last year, Holden reported on alleged maltreatment of some Palestinian prisoners in Israel, claiming most of them were tortured by us. Not true! The Sunday Times needed to know that. President Sadat had ordered the killing of David Hudson should he arrive in Cairo, following his April visit with the British foreign secretary. It was an opportunity for us to send a strong message to the Sunday Times. We're used to people like Hudson, but people like Holden cause more damage to Israel. So go back home and close your farcical investigation. Tell the Sunday Times and your bosses anything you like; the only evidence you have is that Holden was killed by Egyptians."

The "boss" then left suddenly, gesturing that Campbell should be returned to the hotel. Campbell, again blindfolded, was taken back to the location of her abduction. Gibson was already there, left on the side of the deserted road and the first person Campbell saw once the blindfold was removed. They hugged, glad they both survived this ordeal, but Campbell kept quiet and didn't tell Gibson exactly what had happened to her on the short walk back to the hotel. Khalid would have arrived there about two hours before. It was time to go.

At the hotel the two women said goodbye to each other, passionately, promising to stay in touch and keep what had happened between them a secret. Gibson said she'd probably go to Cyprus, the Turkish side, to visit a friend and maybe settle there for a few months. They never met each other again. Campbell rushed to the hotel, packed her stuff, asked Khalid to change her ticket and Adnan to order her a taxi to the airport. She took the first plane to London out of Amman, crashing out in her aisle seat to sleep, exhausted but alive. Strangely disappointed, she gradually realised, not to have seen Youssef in Cairo.

*

Ashraf Marwan, the name that Campbell hadn't recognised from Jawhar's recent testimony, was Nasser's son-in-law but a double agent working for Mossad. After the murder, he was resting in a hotel room in London, talking to his Mossad handler on the phone.

"Why trick us, Daniel? You had us kill the wrong man!"

"Does that matter to you?"

"Our people are panicking in Cairo, we don't know what to do now; the timing was not right, what do we do?"

"You need to do what we normally do. Smear the reputation of the victim, deflect blame away from you; make it look like the work of another agency, as long as you don't point to us, use your imagination."

Marwan put the receiver down, then dialled a Cairo number. "Listen carefully," he said. "You need to do this urgently. Take Colonel Youssef away from the investigation, better if you promote him so he keeps his mouth shut, then dig deep into the past of this dead journalist... find some skeletons. In the meantime, put a few cars around to make it look like it was the work of a foreign agency, until the whole thing fizzles away and dies with him."

PART 3

21

May 1979 – London

As she looked out the window of her Muswell Hill property, watching the bright orange cones get unloaded in readiness for the next set of roadworks, Campbell reflected on the upheaval of the past two years.

The peace treaty between Egypt and Israel was finally signed, Holden would probably have approved of it. A step in the right direction, maybe. A small step, at least, for Palestinians to become fully-fledged Israeli citizens in a single state eventually. This was a solution Holden actually believed in but had never shared widely; only a few knew his views on the subject.

Many more theories about Holden had come out since 1977; that he was a spy for almost half a dozen foreign agencies, a double agent, that his killing was the settling of an old score. Even some of his Sunday Times colleagues started to wonder if these theories had merit. There were inmates in prisons in many parts of the world, including Britain, claiming they knew who killed Holden; they sprung up at an average rate of one a month. Campbell read about these theories, but never paid them any attention. She remembered Holden's phrase: "turning up the decibels in the Tower of Babel". Besides, she'd moved on.

After separating from Stephen, Campbell had come to terms with her bisexuality. She was happy. It was almost the 1980s now, a new decade beckoned, Britain had its first woman prime minister, and Campbell was ready to explore the world. "I want to deal with ordinary cases and ordinary people", she told Snell; so when he offered her the chance to investigate the death of a teacher, Blair Peach, she accepted. Peach died in hospital a day after attending an anti-racism demonstration in Southall. Campbell had become interested in the issue of institutionalised racism within the police force. She wanted to find out more about it. It was a simple issue for her, perhaps clearer too. But she quickly made enemies inside the force; asking difficult questions, requesting interviews with people who she should have left alone. So her new boss was pleased to pass on this message to her: "I was contacted by your old boss, Snell, this morning. They need you to go to West Germany... urgently."

"What?"

"Yeah ... Don't ask *me*, but I think something came up on one of your old cases... the Holden murder, does that makes sense?" Campbell was stressed. She'd told Snell that she didn't want to be involved in the Holden case anymore. All this chasing of wild theories and shadows was disheartening to her, she never again wanted a case in which she knew who the killers were but could not access justice. And why West Germany?

When she met with Chief Superintendent Raymond Snell, he jumped straight to the point. "We need you to go to Pullach, near Munich, in West Germany, there's a chap you need to meet."

"But I'm not working on the Holden case anymore, you know that!"

Snell then explained the background... that earlier that year, an East German double agent had crossed the border into West Berlin and brought with him a pile of confidential documents. Werner Stiller was a young physicist, working for the East German Ministerium für

Staatssicherheit, better known as the Stasi, or HVA, the most notorious foreign intelligence service in the world. He decided to defect to the West, broke a safe to take out a fake exit visa, walked through the checkpoint at Berlin's Friedrichstrasse and boarded the subway to West Berlin. Stiller's job at the Stasi had been to recruit spies from West Germany. When he defected, he took with him a pile of Stasi documents including a microfiche reel of highly sensitive material. One document, Snell told her, might be of particular interest to her.

Although Campbell feared this was just another attempt, rather delayed, to create a new smoke screen around the Holden case to hide the failure in finding his real killers, the presence of a document which she "must" read hooked her. This could be evidence, and she immediately recalled her last "private" meeting with Ruth Holden, after she'd returned from Amman. Ruth had been devastated to learn that her husband's murder was the result of mistaken identity. "Mossad wanted to get rid of your husband but didn't want to get their hands dirty, so they tricked the Egyptians into doing it, killing two birds with one stone if you'll excuse the insensitive pun." Campbell winced at the memory of what a stupid thing to say that was. To tell someone that their loved one was killed is bad enough, but to tell them they were killed by mistake is far worse. Worse still when you tell them that you actually know who the killers are but can't prove it is almost unbearable. Campbell had thought of giving Ruth the usual lines: "enquiries are still ongoing and we hope to bring the killers to justice...", that it was a "difficult case", that "some cases do take years", and all those empty clichés. Campbell did hope, however, that someone might one day confess to killing Holden, or evidence might be found. Would it be in the form of a microfiche reel?

Campbell took the flight to Munich.

A West German police officer met her. "My name is Karston Koenig, from the Special Unit of Bundesnachrichtendienst. Welcome to Germany." The distance from Munich's airport to Pullach was short, and Koenig used all of it to tell Campbell about Stiller. That this was the biggest breakthrough in their fight against the communist East Germany and a victory for the "free world". He also told her that there were many British colleagues already there, working with them. Campbell didn't react, she wasn't keen to meet any of the MI6 guys anyway, especially here in Germany, and her case wasn't espionage ... *unless*, she thought, *Holden really had been a spy all along*. This intrusive thought kept popping up in her head every now and then.

Instead, she kept quiet and listened to Koenig. When they arrived at the Bundesnachrichtendienst HQ she was taken through a long process of jurisdiction paperwork, an interview, a mug shot, security vetting, and a long wait for security clearance. Why had they not sent a copy of the document over to her in Britain and saved all of them time and energy? "I don't know," said Koenig when the DCI voiced the question. "It certainly would have been easier to everyone, but you might know the reason when you read the document."

Campbell was then taken to a dark room with a table, chair and a table lamp, the sort of windowless rooms used for interrogation she thought. A female guard was sitting near the table, and on the table was a plastic folder with some papers inside. Koenig asked her to empty her pockets, gave her a lecture on the dos and don'ts – including only using the pencil and paper provided by them to make notes – he then left her to read the document alone. Campbell nodded a greeting to the guard sat on the chair and took out the document from inside the folder.

It was only two pages and written in German. Actually, Campbell had studied German in college but languages were not her strength. So she was relieved to see, attached to each page, typed translations.

```
Reference: M/77/8/32658
Date: 3rd August 1977
```

Comrades,

This is to inform you that Sonny has sanctioned Operation Ganymede to commence implementation by HVA.

It is important to emphasize that the chronicler is liquidated, preferably in a neutral country so as not to give any leverage to the West.

It is also important to stress that the old item, which Ganymede has obtained from his old master, be recovered and destroyed instantly. Please ensure no strings or traces are left behind.

Wishing you the best of luck with this endeavour in serving the cause of unity of all the workers in the world.

Regards

Comrade T.

22

Campbell didn't know what to make of the document, it was riddled with hints and puzzles which could lead her in any formation of new hoops and circles. She'd been through all this before. *Damn it.* Just as she thought she was going to get clear evidence of some sort, all she got was a riddle that reminded her of the treasure hunt games she used to play with her friends. The only thing she could seize on was the phrase "eliminate a chronicler," which could be a translation error and mean "reporter" or "journalist". That, and the date of the document being August 1977. Campbell thought carefully about the reference to a "neutral place" and she did agree that it looked like it could be to do with Holden specially, that it could explain the timing of the murder. But why the KGB? And why order the HVA to "eliminate" him? And what was the "old item" that Holden had in his possession from his "old master"? All these were questions that Campbell struggled with, so she asked Koenig as she was leaving the reading room if she could meet the defected double agent, Stiller, in person.

"It's impossible, Campbell, I'm sorry. He is being debriefed by several agencies and it is too dangerous for him to meet you. There will be too many approvals required, so forget it Campbell. Use whatever material you have and think about going back to London. I can take you back to the airport now if you are ready?"

"I am not leaving until I meet him, Karsten," said Campbell standing her ground. He did not doubt that Campbell meant what she said, so he agreed to enquire. Campbell had to wait.

Koenig returned from a meeting with his superior after two hours. "Okay, you will be allowed to meet him for 15 minutes, no more, fully supervised and on one condition," Koenig said. "You will not be able to see his face, it would be too dangerous for him at this stage."

Within half an hour the interview was set up. She entered a room, was blindfolded and then sensed a group of men walk into the room. A translator started the conversation by telling Campbell that she had 15 minutes and must ask her questions fast. The DCI wasted no time, but she had to think about her questions very carefully so not to waste the time allotted to her.

"Were you aware of the killing of a British journalist called David Holden in Egypt in late 1977?" asked Campbell loudly as if she was acting in a play. Her clear voice maybe compensating for her lack of vision. The translated answer came back to her:

"I recall I was in a briefing with the big boss, Markus Wolf, about 18 months ago, around the summer of 1977, and there he talked to one of my colleagues about preparing a plan for an operation which I believe involved the killing of a British journalist... but don't know anything else other than that."

"Any idea why that might have been? Did it sound perhaps urgent at the time?"

"The only thing I remember is that yes it did sound urgent, and he did mention a neutral country, so when shortly afterwards I heard David Holden was killed in Egypt on the news, I made the connection. It is my guess by the way, nothing more."

"Who was 'Sonny' as mentioned in the document?"

"Are you asking me this? Really? He's *your* man in *Moscow*." Then after a pause he added, "Mr. Kim Philby."

*

Campbell left Munich for London with nothing but jumbled clues. She hadn't been allowed copies of the documents, but had made notes.

- Stasi HVA operation called for "Operation Ganymede" who is Ganymede?
- Date: 3rd August 1977 (why this date?).
- Eliminate Ganymede the chronicler (Holden? Journalist? Why use the word eliminate?).
- Obtained old evidence from his old master (must find out who the old master is).
- Sonny sanctioned the operation (Stiller thinks this is Kim Philby in Moscow).
- Neutral place (neutral to who? Egypt? Why not Jordan?).

Back in London, Campbell briefed Snell, who was just as puzzled as she was. He promised to contact his old mate, Maurice Oldfield, the ex-head of MI6 and make enquiries. "Maybe he can help," said Snell. In the meantime, Campbell made a plan of action, to know everything there was to know about Holden the man, the reference to an "old master" made her think that Holden may have had a 'past' that she didn't explore, and that this was where she should start. So Campbell decided to meet with his widow and his elder brother all over again, ask them what they knew. But suddenly she received an urgent call from Snell. "The old man, Oldfield, wants to meet you!"

"Never! Not Old Smiley?" Campbell was alluding to Oldfield being the muse for John le Carré's George Smiley novels. It was a nickname by which everyone knew him at that time. "Why?" Campbell asked.

"He said he might be able to help you, he also insisted on meeting you alone, in a café somewhere. He's going to send me over the details," Snell said, as though his DCI had no say in the matter.

Two days later, so not quite as urgent as Snell had suggested, Campbell went to meet Oldfield in a nondescript café near Victoria Station in Central London. After some small talk, she asked him how he might be able to help her with the Holden case. "Actually that was a white lie, just to get to meet you. I need you to help me! I'm talking to you in a semi-official capacity. I actually left *Six* a few months ago, but I'm now off to Ireland on a special task…" he said genuinely whilst Campbell gave him a cynical look. He continued, "Look, I think we can help each other."

"We? Anyway before I make any promises, is Six involved in Holden's murder? Or was he mixed up with Six? Are Harold Evans and his merry men at the Sunday Times telling us the whole truth…?"

"First, let me put your mind at ease in this regard… Holden was never involved with MI6 or any other government agency, as far as we know anyway. He was not recruitment material for us and we weren't interested in him. But it is true that the Sunday Times crowd contacted us after you asked them for copies of the telexes relating to Holden's murder, they discovered that the telexes had disappeared altogether! So they suspected someone inside their team might be a spy. Instead of telling you, they asked us to investigate."

"And? Did you find out who took them?"

"No investigation needed, it was us!" said Oldfield "Six were responsible for the disappearing telexes, but we pretended to the Sunday Times lot that we were investigating."

"MI6 spying on Holden? Why? Why steal those telexes?"

"Not really spying, no, in the past maybe we would have done so, but not now… not until we came to understand that the Soviets were interested in Holden before he died, we just had no idea why. They were watching him, so we watched them watching him. We took copies of the telexes, but only the copies, we never intercepted any."

"Woah woah, hang on! You were running a parallel investigation on Holden and it never occurred to you to tell us this vital piece of information when we were investigating?"

"Because you were doing stunningly well on your own! Better than any of us could've done! We watched you! Besides, we didn't believe that this information was that vital at the time. No one believed that the Soviets had anything to do with Holden… not until this Stiller guy came into the picture."

"I'm sorry Oldfield, I don't buy that!" answered Campbell.

"Hear me out, Campbell, you feisty thing … you see, there's history with Holden…. he received a letter from Kim Philby, directly from Moscow, in August 1966. It made us wonder at the time if it had any code in it. We didn't know at first that George Blake had escaped from prison a couple of months before that letter. We always knew that Holden had known Philby from his days in Lebanon, back in the late 1950s. Holden was a promising young hack back then; just started with the Sunday Times. But later we were sure that Holden was never a spy for anyone and left him alone. Until out of the blue, we learned that the Soviets were interested in Holden again, while he was working on his book on the Saudi royal family. We don't know why exactly."

"So how do you want me to help you?" asked Campbell, not feeling much the wiser, even though the story was interesting.

"Help us by focusing on Holden only and not on any others." Oldfield looked ready to finish the meeting. "Stick to your brief, Campbell, don't wander off."

"Is this a request? Or an order?" asked Campbell.

"I'd better make a move now. I am running late for my train. It was a pleasure meeting you, I feel like you put me though my paces. Bloody impressive… I suspect we might meet again." As Oldfield rose from his chair he added, "Regarding Ganymede, brush up on your Greek mythology and I'm sure you'll get there." And again, as Old Smiley was leaving the café he called out, *"Remember,* Campbell, people aren't *always* what they seem."

Campbell resigned herself to starting new research on David Holden from the beginning, much earlier in his life. She knew David and Ruth Holden were married relatively late in life, in 1962. So she decided to go back even further. This time she was not just going to be led by evidence, this time she would want to know everything about Holden and only then make up her mind what the evidence was. Colchester, and older brother Reginald Holden, was her first port of call.

*

"I had a feeling that you might call, please come in," Reginald said as he opened the door to Campbell and invited her in.

"Yes? Why's that?"

"You haven't found my brother's killers for two years now, so I figured you might start digging up his past."

"I need you to tell me everything about David, Mr. Holden, or rather all about your family background generally."

"So, let me get this right…" the surviving Holden adopted a change in tone that Campbell felt uncomfortable with. He ran his tongue around his lips and regarded a whiskey glass as though all answers were there. "You couldn't find his killers; we've had every Tom, Dick and Harry speculating about the craziest theories; is he a spy, isn't he a spy, maybe a double agent…? Now you have the …well, shall we call it temerity or desperation… to come digging into his past to see which theory fits?" Reginald, she remembered, was a prosecution lawyer. He paused to look intently at the expression on Campbell's face and half-smiled. Then he added, "Ignore my facetiousness, what exactly do you want to know, Detective Chief Inspector?"

"Mr. Holden, I appreciate your frustration, and you have every right to be angry, but I assure you I don't get influenced by these wild theories. I am led by evidence. You of all people should know how we operate."

"Fine, please sit down and tell me where the evidence puts us all now."

"The evidence, the clearest we've had actually but only just come to light, is pointing to David having been killed because of an historical matter. I mean way back in his life… and it would help if you could give me an overview of your family background."

23

"39 Barnes View, Sunderland! That's where David and I grew up," Reginald began. "As I said, we were a typical middle-class Geordie family." Actually, Barnes View was then considered an affluent area. Reginald told Campbell that their life had mainly circled around their father, Thomas Shipley Holden, who was a great influence on both of them. Their mother, Ethel, was a typical English mother upon which the whole household depended. Their father came to Sunderland before they were born, during the Great War, and they grew up remembering nothing but their immediate area. The Holdens were living in a bliss that even World War Two didn't much interrupt. Their father joined the Home Guard, the mother was helping too with other housewives during the Sunderland Blitz, evacuating children from the city. Reginald, the elder, had to interrupt his law degree at university to join the RAF for five years. As for David, he joined a well-known school, Great Ayton Friends, a Quaker school, in 1939 at the start of the war. And he continued his education until the end of the war, before he went up to Cambridge to study Geography.

"David led a school music group during the war, he also formed music groups in school listening to gramophone records every Sunday evening. Just before the war, the school hosted nearly 40 Jewish refugees from Austria, all of them fleeing the Nazi regime. This affected David a great deal and was perhaps his first real life encounter with the 'Jewish Problem'.

"David was the life and soul of our house, especially for our mum and dad. He was energetic and was great company," said Reginald. "I'm glad they'd both gone before he was killed in this way."

He then told her that they were both very close before the war, but when Reginald was called up to join the RAF, the two brothers drifted apart a little. Reginald suggested to Campbell that she contact David's best friend from school, a local man, John Watson. He gave her his details. He'd seen him at David's funeral and so knew he was still around.

*

It took Campbell no time to find John Watson who was pleased that his knowledge of Holden might become relevant to the police as he told her of his school and university memories. They had stayed in touch, despite the war going on around them. Campbell noticed from the various anecdotes that there was a "lack of female company" in Watson's narrative. It made her wonder. There was never a mention of a girlfriend, so she decided to ask a personal question, directly.

"Are you married Mr. Watson? Or have you ever been?"

"No, why do you ask?" answered Watson quickly.

"Nothing in particular, just wondered… the lack of women in the photos in your living room?" She felt that she had probably upset Watson, touched a nerve, but it didn't take long for Watson to tell Campbell that he was "queer". He used that word, even though in the 1970s the word "gay" was widely used. So Campbell decided to venture further and ask him about Holden.

"Did Holden have girlfriends during his school years?"

"Why don't you just ask me if Holden was queer too?"

"Okay, was he? I need to cover all angles. Were you in a relationship with him? Please forgive my asking but this could be important."

"We? Both together? Never! You see I never came out about my sexuality until many years after, in the late 1960s when homosexuality became legal," he said. "Though it was obvious to everyone that I was queer. David and I never talked openly about this, we kept pretending during our years in university that we were far too intellectual to bother with women, but deep down I always had a hunch that David was queer too," continued Watson. "After the war, David dropped a metaphorical bombshell of his own and told me that he wanted to be a professional actor."

"Why was that a shock?" asked Campbell.

"He was always active in drama classes and took part in many school plays… and the school orchestra… he played the clarinet too, but… to pursue an acting career? His father would never have approved." Watson then explained that David's father had great expectations for his son's future, especially in journalism, so for David to pursue an acting career, was a huge shock. "You see professional acting was considered a big risk, especially when you leave a Cambridge degree to pursue such a low key and uncertain career."

"You still haven't answered my question though," said Campbell.

"I am coming to that, Detective Chief Inspector. Nothing is straight forward with Holden, to become an actor in those days, after the war, was considered to be 'soft', so Holden promised his father to become a teacher and take up acting as a hobby."

"When did David start teaching?"

"He taught at Berwickshire High School in a town called Duns near the Scottish borders back in 1947. A geography teacher; very popular with the students. He also he joined a local theatre acting group, Byre Theatre, and took on many of its lead roles. He even made some local headlines at the time, such an excellent performer! But his father was rattled. So he pushed David to get a scholarship and do his Masters, which he also did. Little did he know…" Watson stopped.

"What? What didn't he know? Mr. Watson? What happened?"

"All I know is that when Holden went to study for his Master's in Education Studies in the USA, his scholarship was arranged by a man he'd met here in Britain; older than him, I mean around ten years older! A German Jew if my memory serves me right. That man was already a lecturer in Illinois and managed to convince Holden to join him. Not many people know this by the way."

"Do you know the name of that older man?" asked Campbell.

"Yes. Professor Leo Silberman. He came to Britain in the 1930s fleeing Germany. David met him when he – Silberman – was doing research on Liverpool schools in the late 1940s. They seem to have formed a relationship beyond that of a student learning from an older master…"

"Ganymede!" said Campbell suddenly. She'd checked her Greek mythology and Ganymede had a homosexual relationship with "an older man" – the god Zeus – much to the jealously of Zeus's wife. Campbell started to make some sense of the East German document now. Including the old master reference.

"Ignore me for now," said Campbell looking at Watson' reaction. "I will explain later! Was that gentleman gay? Were they involved? Together?"

"I had my own doubts about them of course. But rumour had it the two were lovers, although the older gentleman had already been married at one point, to a German communist too, as I understand it."

"Did you ever talk to Holden about this? I mean later in life?"

"Well, in those days we didn't talk about these things as openly as people do now. But after we finished school and when we used to meet between his many visits to the Middle East, David always bragged about his relationships with women, he was a very attractive man you know, but you get hunches about these things."

"So, David used to talk about women to you?"

"Maybe to throw me off the scent? When he wrote to me he could easily formulate a misleading narrative. We met only occasionally... Holden never admitted anything to me even though he could have and he knew I would have had no problem with it, he guessed I was queer anyway." Watson seemed ready to leave it there but then added. "Speak to his work mate Jan Morris; she'll tell you more."

Campbell left her meeting with Watson genuinely astonished – she could not believe she hadn't asked all these questions before. Now she felt that she was investigating the murder of a different man. Campbell felt chastened and even a little embarrassed to remember that the Egyptians had been open minded enough to open an investigation into a possible sexual motive. At the time, she'd ridiculed it. Now she knew first-hand that human sexuality was too complex to be compartmentalised... perhaps Holden was, like her, bisexual too? Could human sexuality even be transient, changing with time? Oldfield's parting riddle, that "people are not always what they seem", made perfect sense now. And it's true, Kim Philby was notorious for targeting gay men when recruiting agents, or rather blackmailing gay MI6 agents to become double agents for the KGB. Campbell recalled Harold Evans telling her about Holden's blasé reaction when the Sunday Times covered the Philby's affair. He'd said in a nostalgically black and white manner – oh how her universe had shifted – "quite frankly I am gobsmacked. Back in 1967 when we exposed the level of Philby's damage to MI6, Holden didn't utter a word to us that he knew Philby in Beirut back in the 1950s. *Hmmph*, make of that *what you wish*, I say, Detective Chief Inspector."

24

Campbell found Morris more open and forthcoming this time when she discussed Holden's sexual past. Probably the passage of two years since they had last met convinced her that Holden's past needed to be revisited. The two became drawn close like two schoolgirls who had shared a secret. But Morris had a special charm. "Have you ever thought about why so many young men left Britain after the war?" Morris asked Campbell, before answering the question herself. "True, many wanted to earn more money, that of course, and Britain was practically bankrupt after the war, but some were looking for sexual freedom too, and believe it or not, the Arab world had more tolerance to homosexuality than anywhere else back then."

Morris then recalled how she and Holden became friends when she was 'James', to all intents and purposes a lifetime ago. "It started in November 1956. We were part of some British contingent covering the Suez crisis in Cairo. Nasser had provoked the Egyptians into an anti-British frenzy, to the point where even to look like a European, let alone have fair hair, was like having a target on your back. We were young back then and Holden had come with The Times newspaper, before he joined The Guardian. He, in all innocence, made a trip to Ismalia to witness the arrival of the British troops there. He went alone with an Egyptian journalist and a photographer, but they were arrested and put in prison. Holden told me how he was sickened with fear at that moment, but after a few days the Egyptians cleared him and brought him to join the rest of us and detained us together."

"Where? In another prison?" asked Campbell.

"No, in Semiramis Hotel in Cairo! It was a wonderful hotel at the time, we were all practically prisoners in the hotel at that time. The whole British journalist contingent were almost all the same age, young and inexperienced and there is nothing like fear for binding people together, and add blackouts to the mix! We spent a few weeks together in that hotel and it made us all best of friends. There were many of us but I cannot remember all their names now."

"So what exactly happened in Semiramis Hotel, between the two of you?" asked Campbell without wasting time and Morris was taken aback by the directness of her question.

"Hey, nothing, as far as… did you find something in David's papers or did anyone tell you anything?" asked Morris, hesitating, while Campbell looked sternly at her. Morris continued. "Look… David was a good-looking man, of course I was attracted to him. But only as Jan, not as 'James': Jan was still deep inside me even at that time but hadn't fully come out yet. I felt Holden was attracted to me too, and something inside me knew that he was probably gay, women sense these things as you know. So I hesitated at first, because I was worried that he liked me as 'James', the person I didn't want to be, rather than as "Jan". But then we started to talk. We confided in each other, during that time in Semiramis, that's all."

Morris sensed this wasn't enough for Campbell.

"We became very close and kept in close contact with each other. Holden told me lots of stuff, but forgive me, I'll be keeping it private, even after his death!"

"Even though sharing it might help catch his killers?"

"Ouch, harsh! Nothing Holden told me during this time would

help you, except…" Campbell lifted her eyebrows. "Holden also told me in Semiramis Hotel during the Suez Crisis that earlier he met an older gentleman, a scholar and an interesting character… captivating according to David. I think they became involved."

"Do you mean Professor Leo Silberman?" asked Campbell.

"Yes that's him, he was a mysterious character, most enigmatic. David told me that the best years of his life were when the two of them lived in the US in Illinois, before splitting up. When we talked, Holden confessed that he missed him badly and wished he could convince him to come over and join him in the Middle East."

"And…?" Campbell just wanted to get a move on. She'd waited long enough for the breadcrumbs she was being thrown.

"And that's it really! David and I hardly talked about this subject until one day, we met by chance in 1961 in Jerusalem, it was still under Jordanian rule back then. He told me that Silberman had suddenly died the year before, young at 45, and Holden was distraught about it."

"When was the last time you were in contact with Holden? I mean apart from the postcard."

"Around a month before his death… we bumped into each other by chance at the paper."

"Did he say anything out of the ordinary?"

"Nothing. Something about a big scoop he was working on, which I assumed to mean his new book on the House of Saud, he'd published a series of articles on Saudi Arabia at that time… hang on… you reminded me of something which might be relevant… he also told me that he found some interesting historical information which could explain a lot of things that had happened in the past! Something to do with a document Silberman obtained from a man we knew in the Middle East."

"Name?" asked Campbell.

"A man called Adrian Rivett, we'd both met him in Lebanon.

"Did he say anything else?"

"That's all I recall at this moment."

Campbell went back to her apartment, opened a bottle of wine and mulled everything over. She even thought about Greek mythology again… how she'd opened Pandora's box.

25

May 1979 – Cairo

Over a year ago, Nabil Hassan Ali Youssef was promoted from the rank of Colonel to Brigadier, putting him in charge of President Sadat's ceremonial security unit; a reward, seemingly, for his performance during the Holden investigation, even though he didn't make a single credible arrest, let alone find the killers. Still, President Sadat was impressed with him. Something about Youssef reminded him of himself when he was a young army officer, as he kept saying to his wife, Jehanne.

Saira was expecting their second child and his marriage was still a happy one. He enjoyed fatherhood and that he could now talk with his son and get cute, often very funny, replies. But beyond the domestic, Youssef was a man tormented. A deep sense of shame tore at his soul. His promotion was undeserved. The same conclusion had been reached by now-Colonel Faisal, also promoted. But Faisal was also too busy to dwell on the past at this point in his career.

One day Colonel Faisal contacted Brigadier Youssef to tell him something interesting. "There's a prisoner you should meet, Brigadier," said Faisal. "He says he knows something about the murder of that Englishman David Holden, and... listen to this... he is a policeman. He's one of us!"

"Right... What is he in for?" asked the judgmental Youssef.

"Selling arms to a Palestinian group, but this has nothing to do with Holden."

"Have you interrogated him?"

"He wouldn't talk, sir, he insisted he would only talk to you."

"I'm on my way!" he answered.

Youssef knew better than to get excited by tips from colleagues, he got them every day and most came to nothing. But the fact that the man Faisal mentioned was actually a policeman was an interesting fact. Youssef always suspected that someone in the Egyptian police was involved in Holden's murder, one way or another. This fitted well with his suspicions, so his interest was piqued.

He didn't bother getting permission from his boss. He didn't think that he needed it or that it was even worth bothering the President with a triviality like this. So he headed to what was his old office, the state security department at Madinat Nasr, and met Faisal there. After the ceremonial hand salutes, accompanied with rising dust in the room from stomping feet, Faisal said: "This man is different from the rest!"

This man was Awad Muhammed Abdul-A'atti. He was 37 and a sergeant in the vice squad. His reputation for being bent preceded him wherever he went, as did the general opinion that he didn't have a single moral fibre in his body. Yet it was clear to Faisal, and later to Youssef, that Abdul-A'atti was only a chancer, a mere opportunist who would do anything for money. Pimps, prostitutes, drunks were all in his line of duty. His colleagues had told Faisal that Abdul-A'atti had been given many opportunities for promotion and transfers to other departments but he'd declined them all; a sea of vice was his natural element and the continuous flow of small bribes, from grateful customers, was not to be sniffed at.

"How did he end up here? Who blew his cover?" asked Youssef.

"We caught him one night selling a pistol to a group of Palestinian students. When we checked his past cases we found by chance that he was the first officer at the scene of Holden's murder."

The officers brought Abdul-A'atti to the interrogation room, familiar to Youssef of course. It was more like a school classroom than an interrogation room, in fact it even had a few school desks in it. And the whiteboard was still there. Youssef and Faisal both sat at different desks, waiting for Abdul-A'atti to enter.

When he came into the room he looked haggard in his civilian clothes and was clearly scared. Being caught selling arms to political activists in Egypt was no small affair, a death sentence was not unusual. So Abdul-A'atti hurled himself at Youssef's mercy and told him that he'd confess everything if they let him go free.

"Tell me what you told Colonel Faisal about that Englishman, Holden. Include the most boring details, I am all ears for you tonight." Youssef commanded.

"Sir, I swear all I did was help with putting the body in its resting place, I was not involved in his killing at all. If I tell you what you I know, you promise you'll let me go free?"

"It depends on what you tell us. You know that! But I can promise you that if the information leads us to the killers the charges against you will be reduced to a minimum."

"In February 1977 I met a khawajah, an Englishman, during a raid on an illegal brothel in Ma'adi. He was caught in the act and we took him with all the others to the station at Bab Al-Louq. The man looked European to me and didn't belong with the rest. He stood out. He offered me money to let him go. What can I say? Life was hard on my family, sir, so I took the money and let him go. I knew he'd be let out anyway... tourists caught in brothels always are."

"So? Go on, what happened next?" prompted Faisal.

"After a few months, around September of that year, I bumped into the same man again outside the police station. I think he was waiting for me, even though he pretended it was a coincidence. We spoke and he started to hint that he had some more cash for me, but that it would be a different type of work. Gradually his talk became threatening. He spoke in the plural… that 'they' had evidence against me… and sure enough he showed me pictures of me taking bribes from pimps. It seemed he had people watching me. Life is hard, sir…" Abdul-A'atti said with a wide-eyed shrug. "He offered me large sums of cash in return for providing him with some stolen cars that he wanted placed in certain locations across Cairo at specific times. Then later he offered to pay me more if I also managed to get rid of a body for him."

"And you just said yes?" said Youssef angrily.

"I am going to tell you everything I know, sir, just bear with me a little. At first, he told me some story about an Englishman 'they' wanted to punish because he'd swindled them out of a considerable amount of cash, in England, and run away. He didn't talk about killing at first; that was introduced right at the last minute."

"Last minute? You mean he didn't plan to kill him at first? Think hard before you answer."

"No sir, that's my understanding," said Abdul-A'atti. "The idea of killing the man and getting rid of his body came around a month before the operation. The cash was huge for a man like me. Plus he was blackmailing me, so what choice did I have? I accepted. But, sir, understand this… all I did was take the body and lay it down in some wasteland, nothing else. I know I did something bad but please, I promise I will help you catch this khawajah man."

"How do I know if you're telling us the truth? You probably killed the man yourself."

"Sir, I will tell you what happened and you judge for yourself. You remember the body was laid like this…" Abdul-A'atti described the position of the body exactly as they found it. "And you probably noticed the spectacles were placed crookedly, yes?" Youssef and Faisal nodded "This was because I noticed them at the last minute. I'd been told to remove them and I forgot; but by the time I tried to remove them one of your officers arrived so I panicked, stopped and left them in that state."

"And yet you could have known all this because you were the first officer arriving at the scene," countered Youssef.

"Why do think I would confess to a crime like this, sir?" asked Abdul-A'atti.

"To get away with a far more serious crime, selling arms to a terrorist! You think we are fools?" answered Youssef.

"Yes... I mean no ... sir, bear with me to the end and you judge for yourself. The plan I was told about involved two groups, or gangs if you prefer. I was the leader of one gang, mostly made up from my own criminal contacts, people with whom I'd kept in touch over the years. And there was another gang made up of foreigners whom I only saw once, briefly, in the dark in the early hours of Wednesday 7 December 1977."

"How many in each gang?" asked Faisal.

"My gang had four people including myself, and from what I saw their gang was also four apart from the dead man... Holden. But I think they did have other people working with them behind the scenes. They asked me to steal three Fiat Nasr cars."

Youssef jumped off his seat. "Three cars?"

"Yes sir, three cars and all of them were Fiat Nasr models, one green and two white. I was specifically told to make sure they were 'not too old and not too new', that they'd blend well with the Cairo scene! He was specific about the cars, so I stole the cars for him and hid them in a large derelict warehouse in Helwan." Youssef was still thinking about the third car. Abduction, murder... and?

"And then?" asked Faisal this time. Abdul-A'atti had now hooked both of them into listening to his every syllable.

Then followed details only someone connected closely with the investigation would know, but Youssef still had his suspicions that as a low-key policeman, their man may have heard these details second-hand.

"I was given the signal on the evening of Tuesday December 6th to take the three cars and place each one at a specific location. I can take you there and show you."

"A written account will do. And write down the names of your mates while you're at it." Faisal threw him a pencil and pushed a pad of paper towards him. The resulting account showed a level of planning that had to belong to an organised criminal outfit, as Abdul-A'atti started writing it in steps, with some sketches, for his captivated audience:

Step 1: I drove the green car alone, one of my mates following me in one of the white cars, he was also alone. We went from the warehouse to the airport. I left the green car at an agreed place in a parking lot near the airport. Then I joined my mate as a passenger in the white car and we both continued to an agreed desert location.

Step 2: The other two of my mates, took the third white car from the warehouse to rendezvous with us at the desert location. They parked on the edge of the main desert road and we parked our car around 100m deep into the desert using a dirt track. We left our car in place and then walked to where our mates were waiting in the white car at the main road.

Step 3: Us four stayed inside the white car at the agreed spot on the main road pretending the car was broken down. The first part of our job was now done; all we needed to do was wait for the guys we were now with to finish their part.

Then Faisal, busy with trying to fathom the connections, clarified, "So at that point, the first car is in the airport left empty, the second car is in the desert left empty, and the third car is parked along the desert road, with all four of you waiting, yes?"

Abdul-A'atti smiled in agreement signalling that he had managed to get through to them at last.

"But are you saying you never met the killers? The second gang? The foreigners?" asked Youssef angrily.

"That's exactly what I'm saying, sir. We saw them from a distance but never actually met them. They all looked foreign to me from afar, I mean non-Egyptian, and everything happened so quickly. It was a cold night and dark so we only saw figures of people, silhouettes, we didn't even hear the gunshot when it was fired."

"Liar! You are just playing us for fools. Did you at least see that Englishman... I don't mean the dead one, I mean that khawajah, at the murder scene?" asked Youssef.

"No sir. I swear to you, let me tell you what I saw that night, when it all happened, and you judge for yourself. I ask you to indulge me..." begged Abdul-A'atti. He knew he could be fighting for his life.

"Go on, but be accurate this time," said Faisal. "Tell me every detail and no more lies!" Abdul-A'atti looked at both men and asked them for a break; they brought him a glass of water.

"Sirs, when I was inside that white car with my mates, waiting along the road, we didn't do anything, just stayed put, waiting. After around 40 minutes, we saw a car approaching, a foreign car, a nice large one, black colour, not sure of its make, looked different from any other car I know of. It came slowly and quietly along the road, turned into the dirt track. We saw one man getting out and he jumped into the white car. The large car then pulled back onto the road and disappeared."

"So they dropped someone at the murder scene in the desert area... go on, what happened afterwards?" asked Youssef, thinking that this must be the professional assassin. It was starting to make some sense to him if so.

"Then after about an hour the green car, the same car I'd dropped earlier at the airport, showed up with four people sitting inside it. I later guessed that Holden was one of them, they were sitting like you'd expect, a driver and one passenger up front and Holden and another man in the back. Their car went over the same dirt track and parked close to the other car where that foreign man was waiting. Then three figures opened the doors and pulled Holden away from the airport car, forcing him to go to the other car. We could see that Holden was struggling against them, resisting with all his strength, but we couldn't hear him shouting from where we were. When they were outside the airport car, they handcuffed him and pushed him into the other car, so now there were three people sitting in the front, with Holden in the middle." Abdul-A'atti saw that Youssef and Faisal were barely disguising their excitement.

"Yes, yes! And then?" shouted Faisal.

"At that point there was a total of five men including the English journalist at the murder scene, but all we saw were the remaining two men standing outside waiting by their car, which looked strange to us as it was freezing that night, but the three men inside the other car were still talking... They looked very calm to us to be honest... there was no sign of struggle or anything after that. Then the front passenger lowered his windows, I think he called out to the others and one of them opened the boot of the airport car, and took out a bag, a small one, probably a small briefcase, and gave it to them. We saw the English man opening up the briefcase – by then the dome light inside the car was turned on, or may be there was torch light, I'm not sure – Mr. Holden took out his reading glasses, put them on and took out a piece of paper. They all looked as if they were reading it, then it got handed to one of the guys in the front passenger seat, who also started reading it."

"And then?" asked Youssef.

"And then there was nothing for about ten minutes. We thought maybe the whole thing was resolved. Until there was a split second where one of the two men who were standing outside opened the back door and jumped inside the car… but he kept one foot touching the desert ground outside. He quickly threw away an object, just chucked it outside, stayed like that for a few seconds and that was it, it was done… by that time. The dead Englishman was kept squeezed between the two men in the car, and the remaining four men left the scene. They started walking towards us and signalled to us that the second part of our job had started. We walked in the opposite direction, they jumped into our car parked by the main road and took off with it, and I never saw them or that car after that."

"What did you do?" Faisal felt frustrated that he had to keep chivvying the narrative along. He just wanted to absorb it and think afterwards.

"Then my gang, the four of us, went to the scene of the two cars in the desert. The white car had the dead man inside it and the airport car was parked near it. One of us jumped into the white car while we moved the body back to the airport car."

"Hang on, why? Why not keep the body where it was? Why did they need *two* cars for that?! That doesn't make sense to me!" said Youssef.

"To wash the blood from the murder car, even though there was so little of it as it turned out later, but sirs, it was planned this way. Only after my mate took off with the murder car, I noticed that the object chucked onto the ground was a headrest from the murder car, so I put it inside the green airport car with the body…"

"Why did you not leave the headrest in the desert?"

"Our instructions were to not leave any trace behind, so I took it in the green car, to give me time to think about how to deal with it later… So there are four of us with the dead Mr. Holden, in the desert with two cars. We made him sit upright in the back of the airport car and made him look as if he was sleeping, with his glasses firmly on with his frozen smile. Three of us took the airport car with Holden inside it and went to Darb Al-Ahmar Road, parked the car by a dumpster, and my two mates dropped the body in that place while I waited in the car. Then I drove us home. The other man from our gang took the murder car and went directly to the warehouse, I changed my clothes and started my shift at the police station as normal, making sure I would be the first officer to receive the report about finding the body."

"Did you hear the other men, from the other gang, talking? What language they were using? What did they look like? Give us more details!" shouted Faisal.

"The three people who came with Holden from the airport were, well, one looked dark Nubian, one looked Arab but didn't look like an Egyptian to me, the third one looked Italian. You know tall, dark hair but white, and the fourth who came alone by the large car was foreign looking, with blond hair."

"What about the Englishman behind the operation, the one you busted in the brothel? Do you have a name? Can you meet him again?"

"I never saw him after that, sir, in fact I never saw him during the operation either. Even the rest of the money which was owed to me was dropped off by someone else the next day. It wasn't him who came. I was relieved." Faisal and Youssef looked at each other. But Abdul-A'atti then added, "I do have his name and his passport details," added Abdul-A'atti, sensing a last-ditch chance to avoid execution.

"How?" asked Faisal, hardly believing.

"When we caught him at the brothel, he had his passport on him. I made a note of his details before giving it back to him. Something I always do, actually…"

"What's his name?" Youssef looked stern, but deep down he was rejoicing.

"Barron, sir. Anthony Barron. He had a British passport, but he kept telling me he was Irish. As if I would know the difference!"

26

"I am pleased to inform you that we now have killers of the British journalist, David Holden, in our custody." This was Sadat's announcement to the world the next morning. Youssef hadn't wanted it announced immediately. He'd wanted more time to investigate who exactly Anthony Barron was. But his subsequent research quickly uncovered that there was indeed a British man called Anthony Barron who had come to Cairo in January 1977 and stayed for almost one year. Youssef noticed that the date of his departure from Cairo was Tuesday December 6th, early evening, before Holden's arrival in Cairo, and almost exactly an hour after Holden had got on his plane in Amman. This fitted exactly with Youssef's suspicion that Barron was the organiser of the murder, or, as Campbell would have put it, the organ grinder. And before he knew it, Minister Nabbawi had contacted Scotland Yard in London and Youssef was back in Heathrow to meet once more with Campbell.

In the meantime, Campbell had come out of her meeting with Jan Morris convinced that the clue to solving Holden's murder lay in knowing more about Holden's relationship with Leo Silberman, starting in the late 1940s and continuing into the 1950s. Morris told her two fundamental things: the first being that Silberman's sudden death at 45 in September 1960 may not have been, as officially stated, due to natural causes. The second being that Holden may have stumbled across an important discovery and all signs suggested that he was going to tell Morris about it before his departure to Egypt. Perhaps Holden had changed his mind, thought that it could wait until his return from Egypt. Which implied the new discovery was not so urgent at the time. Campbell had a hunch that this discovery was relevant to Silberman. How can the death of one person in 1960 be connected to the death of another in 1977? Campbell sat in her office, gathering her thoughts. Then her boss, Snell, rang.

"It seems that something new cropped up in Holden's case, in Cairo. Nabil Youssef, he's a Brigadier now by the way, he's on his way to us for help. He is coming to meet us both, Campbell… tomorrow!"

*

The Brigadier and the DCI met each other with the same amount of unvoiced sexual tension. Campbell looked more attractive to Youssef this time, more liberated. Soon his shyness went away and the two began to open up to each other. She whisked him through airport security and in no time he was in her car on the way to the same hotel he'd stayed in two years before.

After Youssef had briefed Campbell and Snell, the English officers felt they'd sat through a protracted précis of a Hitchcock film. Were they about to solve this murder, jointly? Many events were happening around them at that time, at the forefront was the news about the Iranian Revolution; Shah Pahlavi leaving Iran and settling in Cairo. But as soon as Youssef mentioned the name "Anthony Barron" to them, Snell immediately thought he'd heard the name before.

"Campbell," he said, clicking his fingers quickly. "You remember the prison siege in Scheveningen in Holland back in 1974? A man with the same name, Tony Barron, cabled the Dutch police to the effect that he could help them end the siege, remember?" Campbell tried to recollect. Snell continued. "The Dutch Police asked us to do a background check on him at that time, but we had little on him; he was a paratrooper during the war, served in Holland, and was under the watch of Special Branch. We thought of him more as a conman or some sort of showman, who bragged about being in the SAS with all his cloak and dagger antics."

"Yes, I remember now, it was so strange…" said Campbell. "And one of the four convicts who carried out the siege was a Palestinian, who was serving a sentence in the Netherlands for hijacking a plane from Bombay to London… there may be a connection." Snell requested of his secretary a report on Tony Barron and the three continued discussing the latest information they'd received from Youssef. Snell's secretary came back to the room and put a sheet of paper in front of the Chief Superintendent.

"Well, well, well… what do you know…? Tony Barron is currently an inmate in Brixton prison. How convenient is that!" Snell added, "you two better go right now and talk to him."

Campbell hadn't had a chance to share with Youssef anything yet; she didn't even have a chance to tell him about Werner Stiller, nor did she tell him about Professor Leo Silberman. It all seemed of secondary importance to Youssef's discovery of Barron's connection. She had to agree that the confession and testimony of Abdul-A'atti was the greatest breakthrough in the case. To Campbell's mind, Abdul-A'atti had to be the man with the scar that had so scared Bilal Ibrahim, the third-year medical student whom she met in Cairo. But Campbell didn't say anything to Youssef about her adventurous visit to Cairo, still thinking that the Egyptian police might, just might, be behind the murder.

At Brixton Prison, Barron looked more frail than Campbell had imagined him. She knew he'd be in his mid-fifties now, but he looked so much older. He was "in" for armed robbery. They both knew they were dealing with a common criminal, not an ideological thinker; an opportunist who was trying to make quick money and publicity out of any situation. So Campbell suggested to Youssef that they needed to be careful not to believe everything or even anything Barron told them. He was, simply put, an attention seeker.

No surprise then that he spoke first. "I will only talk to you off the record, madam… Salaam… sir," said Barron. Campbell after some hesitation put her notepad and pen to the side and ejected the tape from the small recorder she'd brought with her. "Thank you," said Barron. "How can I be of help?" That was when Youssef told Barron how they'd caught Abdul-A'atti and about his confession.

Barron listened attentively to every word Youssef said, in his clear but somewhat broken English. Finally, Barron showed he grasped the importance of the issue with his dry reply. "It wasn't exactly a brothel actually, it was a floating boat on the Nile, with a casino and a few women with loose morals. I didn't know anything about it being illegal, but anyway what he told you is largely correct."

They asked Barron about how he got involved in organising Holden's murder. Barron told them that he'd come to Egypt to "try his luck", with Egypt's openness to the West he'd managed to submit some bogus reasons for a visa by early 1977. "I was approached by a West German gentleman in Cairo, someone I met by coincidence at the bar in the Shepheard Hotel – not the old vintage one, the new one – anyway, he said his name was Franz Schmidt and that he was a businessman, working in Egypt to promote some project or other. But he looked as if he had some status in Egypt, and we got talking; and became sort of friends. He told me some interesting war stories, then he started asking me for a few favours, nothing serious but teetering on the edge of legality in a country like Egypt. I had a British passport with me and so wasn't worried. I had my contacts in Egypt too. I think now he was testing me to see if I could come up with the goods. And I did. Every time."

"What kind of favours?" asked Campbell.

"Things like forging currency transactions, forging business visas from British embassies from around the world, forging stamps, getting stolen cars, I never asked him why, but I did them for him."

"Who helped you?" asked Youssef.

"Oh? Did Abdul-A'atti omit that part?" He continued, "anyway, as we built up trust between us, he asked me for more errands and was paying good money on results, US dollars by the way. The errands started to get more serious every time, this is for most of the first half of 1977," said Barron.

"Tell us about the serious ones!" ordered Campbell.

"I will tell you everything but let me make one thing clear from the outset… when Schmidt, or whatever his real name was, asked me to help him organise the Holden operation, he didn't give me the name. All he told me was that he was a frightened man running away from some people, powerful people, that he owed money to. He didn't even say it would lead to killing him either, come to think of it. Though he floated it as a possibility, in case Holden resisted or did something stupid. Whatever stupid meant. It was only a possibility at that point, barely that. I didn't ask any more questions anyway, so my role was limited to organising the operation. I helped with the logistics only. I did not have anything to do with his death, certainly not."

"You think that makes you less culpable?" asked Youssef. Barron looked at Youssef but chose to ignore him and turn his head toward Campbell.

"Madam, I was desperate for money and I accepted. I needed to find some low-life murdering types in Egypt and I didn't know any. Not until I met Sergeant Abdul-A'atti from Vice. He was a bent officer and just the right man for the job. Remember, I didn't know that the man in question was Holden at first."

"Why does that matter? Would you have asked for more money?" asked Youssef sarcastically.

"No. I wouldn't have got involved at all if I have known it was Holden, a fellow Brit. I thought he was another bloody kraut…" Barron continued in a warmer, less clipped voice. "Look, I agreed with Mr. Schmidt ab…."

"Tell us about this man, Schmidt. Is he still in Egypt?" interrupted Youssef. Barron turned to Campbell.

"Please tell your colleague to be civil. I am here helping you voluntarily, and I am as keen as you to know why Holden was killed." Campbell pressed Youssef's arm, signalling to him to ease off, and was only mildly distracted by the warm, firm muscle that met her fingers.

"All I can tell you about Schmidt," said Barron with a sigh, "was that he was perhaps a diplomat or something. He had blond hair and looked young, smooth shaven, his English was very good but with that strong German accent that always transports you to a 1930's Nazi rally. The only condition I made to him was that I had to leave Egypt on the day of the operation. He agreed. The date kept changing though, until it was finally fixed for Tuesday December 6th, at night."

"What was the original date? And when was that date fixed?" asked Campbell.

"Originally the date was December 3rd but later we agreed that we, I mean Abdul-A'atti and his men, would be ready at 24 hours' notice. They asked us to get the cars ready for Sunday November 27th."

"That was the first car, Mr. Barron. The other two cars were stolen on Tuesday 6th, the day of the murder."

"The delay in stealing the other two cars was to do with Abdul-A'atti cutting his risks." Barron smiled at this point. "He only had a secure garage to fit one car. He couldn't steal the other cars and then park them outside waiting, could he?" Barron answered quickly as he could see that both of his interrogators were absorbing his words.

"Then why all this elaborate operation? Why *three* cars?" asked Youssef. Maybe the brigadier was still upset that he'd been proved wrong about the two cars. After all, that theory had been pretty impressive at the time, getting him a lot of kudos.

"That one is on me. I'm the one who divided the operation into three parts, with each part having its own car. I was a paratrooper myself during the war, a young lad, and was involved in a landing operation in no man's land. The first thing our commander did was to split us into smaller groups, each had a task to do, and he prepared us with what to say to the enemy if we ever got caught. Seemed like a good MO to replicate! The first part was the "kidnapping" which involved luring the victim into a car away from the airport…" Youssef made a mental note: abduction car.

"The second part was the "discussion car", which turned out later to be the killing car…"

"Murder car!"

"…and the third was the 'getway car'."

"But," Youssef was rattled beyond what was rational. "Why three cars?"

"To spread our risks. If anything went wrong during the kidnapping part and the guys got caught they could give a simple excuse, like a failed robbery. If however they caught the car during the disposal of the body, they'd have another excuse, something like we found him shot and we're taking him to hospital. Simple really," said Barron but then added, "we expected the murder car would be full of blood and to be disposed off separately from the others."

Hmmm, still… just two cars would have sufficed, thought Youssef, but he knew he had to let it go. "Tell me how many times Schmidt met with you and Abdul-A'atti's men," he asked instead.

"Schmidt never met anyone except me, he never met Abdul-A'atti or his men. This was also part of reducing the risks. People are only accountable for their own parts and what they themselves know." He thought the officers looked impressed. "You can take the man out of the paratroopers, but…" Barron grinned.

Campbell and Youssef left Brixton Prison dazed and exhausted. The amount of information and leads that Barron gave them was huge, yet he didn't really say anything new that Abdul-A'atti hadn't already said to Youssef. But it was good to have had it corroborated in London. Campbell took Youssef back to the hotel, but this time he asked her to come to his room so they could take stock of what Barron had said to them and make a plan, away from the noise of the hotel lobby. She accepted after some hesitation, knowing what might be happening.

And it did happen. She'd been yearning to be touched for so long, without completely realising it. And Youssef was definitely the right man in the right place. Her eyes locked on his again, just as they had the first time they'd met. She recognised in him the man that her husband, Stephen, had never been; a man with a resolute self-containment that held deep within it a desire to please, to do good. A desire that extended into deep connections with those he found attractive. Slightly older than him and distinctly less 'fit', Campbell wondered if there was something maternal about her appeal to the brigadier. Brigadier! Now that was sexy! A brigadier with a tongue that struck at each nipple in turn, his fast breaths landing hard and warm between her breasts as his mouth made its way up to her throat. She was desperate to feel his strong lips on her mouth now, wanted the intimacy. His tongue had already done all the work that was necessary… her body was on fire, almost unbearably so. She just craved his breath and intimacy on her lips now, the closeness of his gentle face.

Youssef was nowhere near as self-assured in his passion as he seemed. His body was ready and he felt the thrill of the promise of relief her hand provided; he focused on extending the moment, turned his head to the side, and thought about anything other than the English woman who was now moving beneath his hips, anticipating his entry. *A dissection of Barron's interview will have to wait for the morning*, he was desperately telling himself. While there was nothing Campbell wanted that wasn't part of Youssef's body. But then something other than strategic distraction hijacked their immediate plan of action. A knock at the door with a message to Campbell from Snell. It read, "Adrian Rivett is now living in Morocco, Tangier, and he is willing to talk to us."

27

By the time Campbell and Youssef had landed in Tangier, the report requested on Rivett was waiting for them at the hotel.

Adrian Harris-Rivett, born 1908, ex-army, had been Captain at the Bedfordshire & Hertfordshire Regiment, and served in Africa during the war where he was decorated with DSO in 1941, court martialled and cashiered from the army in Germany in 1955, imprisoned for one year for gross indecency, leaving Britain after his release and settling somewhere in the Middle East. No further information for after he had left Britain could be found.

Unsurprising. Rivett it turned out was living as a total recluse. They met with him on the day of their arrival, having struggled to get through from his apartment's hallway to his lounge, negotiating the piles of books and magazines on the floor and everywhere. Some were newspaper cuttings in many languages. Clearly a hoarder, and widely read. He had one Somali boy as a servant who came to offer them some cold drinks. But they cut to the chase and asked him about his encounters with Holden in 1950's Lebanon. He was not surprised by the question somehow.

"I first came to Lebanon after I was released from the army, to try my luck, a new life, like many people did at that time in 1956; it was a few months before Eden's folly in Suez. The Nasserist tide was overwhelming the Arab World in those days, spreading like wildfire, especially among the Muslims in Lebanon." Rivett was in no hurry to get to the point. "I became a representative of a Newcastle company in Baghdad, called Mackley & Co, selling mechanical equipment manufactured by the company. They were selling new types of pumps and Iraq had started to boom in the fifties. So I lived between Baghdad and Beirut during this period. In fact I was in Baghdad during the revolution of the summer of 1958 and stayed until I was deported by the revolutionaries. So I relocated back to Lebanon, and stayed there until this civil war broke out a few years ago. I have lived in Tangier since."

"And how is this relevant to David Holden?" asked Youssef impatiently.

"There was a group of us living in Lebanon at that time, we were men but with different inclinations, you might say…"

"Wait, you and Holden were homosexuals?" asked Youssef angrily. Of course, this was news to Youssef as Campbell kept this from him. He was losing interest in this interview already and wanted to leave, but Campbell waved to Youssef, telling him to calm down and let their man continue. So Rivett aimed his next section of autobiography at Campbell.

"… not anymore, you could say I am too old for that now. But in those days, a few western Arabists were attending MECAS in Shemlan in Lebanon, the spy school run by the British Foreign Office. Beirut was full of spies in those days all watching each other, but for our type it was always harder…" Rivett said.

"Why are you telling us all this?" asked Youssef.

"Because you need to know the context of what I am about to tell you," said Rivett.

"Please continue Mr. Rivett," said Campbell.

"The situation got a lot worse in Beirut in the summer of 1958:

many British went back to Blighty, the ones who were left behind were those who didn't have a home to go back to, mostly our type. We had the best time of our lives, meeting in the evenings in the St. George Hotel by the sea, the Chateaubriand Hotel or the Lucullus Restaurant on French Avenue for seafood. Amazing times," said Rivett reflecting. "And the strange thing was that whenever a group of us queers met up, one person, who was not supposed to be one of us, always seemed to pop up out of the woodwork and join us…" Campbell and Youssef wondered why Rivett had trailed off.

"Who was that person?" prompted Campbell.

"Philby, Kim Philby. He was always hovering around British homosexuals which made me wonder about him at the time, though I knew he'd been married three times by then. Still, it did make me wonder… until of course he defected to Moscow in 1963. Only then I guessed he was trying to recruit queers as agents for the KGB, perhaps the ones he could blackmail… homosexuality was illegal in Britain at that time you see… and had a huge stigma attached to it. Many of us, not me by the way, were trapped in marriages… often with children too, so blackmail was effective. I didn't know that Holden was one of us until I met him…"

Youssef was infuriated. "Why are you telling us all this? Why don't you tell us about Holden in 1977 instead?"

"Be patient and listen to me please and you will understand," Rivett answered Youssef in perfect Arabic, but then switched back to English, "I have been agonizing about this ever since I heard about Holden's murder… just wondering… you see after I was kicked out of Iraq I had no means of supporting myself; business was going downhill and the Middle East was always coming out of one turmoil just to jump into another. I had in my possession an old document, an original historical piece of paper, given to me by a tribal chief in Africa during the war. I have been wanting to sell it for some time, until I had to, so I asked the people around me to find me a buyer. One day, probably around May 1960 a man called Bruce Abdurrahman Conde, an American stamp collector, contacted me and told me that he'd found me a buyer for the document."

"Hang on," Campbell interrupted. "What was this historical document?"

"Not much, actually, it was just the original of a simple letter containing nondescript correspondence from a British Governor to an African tribal chief, but it had some seals on top that I couldn't read. The African chief gave it to me during the war in 1940 when I was with the Somali Camel Corps and told me to keep it safe for him... he said it was important. But the chief died shortly after and no one claimed it from me."

"Do you have a copy of it?" asked Campbell.

"Not anymore but I did at one point and I even got it translated. As I said it was a simple letter. I threw all that away few years after I sold it. It did not sound important to me even back then. Anyway, Conde arranged for the buyer to come to my apartment in Beirut and I organised a small gathering of friends, those of us Europeans who'd stayed behind in Beirut in the summer of 1958 with a civil war raging around us. Just as we were waiting for the buyer to turn up, sure enough, Kim and his famous Arabist father, St. John Philby knocked at the door, uninvited as usual. Then came Conde, Holden... and the buyer. He was a middle-aged professor teaching in a university in the USA, or somewhere... had a Jewish name..."

"Leo Silberman," nodded Campbell, alerting Youssef to the fact that he didn't have the full picture. So much for pillow talk!

"Yes, yes! That's it!! You wouldn't believe how I sometimes rack my brains trying to remember that name. Thanks! So we sat in my apartment and after all the niceties and the usual hospitalities, I took Silberman to the balcony and showed him the document. I could see the excitement on Silberman's face when he saw that simple letter, as if he was looking at a treasure only he could appreciate. Then he put it in his briefcase, handed me the agreed cash in US dollars, and we shook hands. I could see Philby looking at us from the inside of the apartment, the whole time we were on the balcony. I guess he knew about the document from Conde, since he and St. John Philby were friends – or friendly rivals would be a better summation. After going back inside the apartment, it was clear to me that Philby was trying hard to get close to Silberman, but Silberman was in a hurry to leave Beirut and get back to Africa."

"Do you think Philby knew Holden? Were they close?" asked Campbell to the frustration of Youssef who felt lost in this weaving together of British spy stories.

"It was during that gathering St. John convinced Holden and Silberman to come with him to visit Arabia, to see it before it changes for ever after the oil. But Silberman left and went to Kenya, while the rest went together with St. John and Kim to visit Saudi Arabia for few weeks. I think Holden did his TV programme on Arabia based on this visit, if I remember rightly. So, you want to know why I'm telling you all this, right?"

"Do you think Holden's murder might be connected to this document?" Youssef was connecting the dots.

"I'm not sure. Silberman died just weeks after he bought the document from me, and I have no idea what happened to it after that," answered Rivett. "This troubles me still. I often wondered if Silberman died because of the document I sold him. Then there'd be a good chance Holden might have been connected to it too somehow."

28

In a Tangier hotel room, Campbell and Youssef went over their research to date. They studied all possibilities and mapped all scenarios in their notepads. But still they went back to Silberman, every time. Having reached a dead end, they decided to fly back to London to find out more about the professor. Youssef had forgiven Campbell for not briefing him about what she knew, which made their conversation easier. But the more they dug the more confusing it became.

This man, Silberman, who died at the age of 45 in 1960, from natural causes, seemed to be nowhere and everywhere. At one point they thought they were dealing with more than one person with the same name. Campbell recalled Watson's description of the man having "intellectual prowess" and it seemed he was right. Silberman was born in 1915 in Darmstadt, south of Frankfurt; the eldest son of resourceful Jewish parents, Fred and Hilda Silberman. Hilda's father was a director of L.S. Mayer, the fancy goods manufacturer. Their youngest son was Freddy Silberman who, unlike his academic brother, followed his father into the business, and was still alive. The whole family had a connection to Africa one way or another. So, when the Second World War broke out, his father whisked his sons away to Johannesburg, out of harm's way. But Leo joined the Free French army in French

Equatorial Africa which refused to be part of Vichy France, and became a pilot.

But he was too clever and curious to be pigeon-holed into anything. He pursued a career path very few people would dare to take, later becoming an expert in many subjects. He first studied sociology at Witwatersrand University in South Africa, and ended up lecturing there and became an expert on the Belgian Congo. He vehemently opposed apartheid and advocated the co-existence of whites with the black majority. He would relish upsetting people around him, especially when he befriended the first black student at Witwatersrand University, a certain Nelson Rolihlahla Mandela.

Soon after the war Silberman came back to Britain calling himself an "urban sociologist" and conducted research on schools in Liverpool. This was where he met Holden. When Silberman had an opportunity to teach in the US, he convinced Holden to follow him.

By now Campbell and Youssef had made up their minds that Silberman was a spy for the KGB, like Philby; his homosexual relationship with Holden might have presented an opportunity for the KGB to recruit the Englishman too.

"Could Silberman have been Holden's handler in the KGB? Did Holden go rogue after Silberman died?" Youssef asked.

"Could be! But why wait 17 years to kill him? In fact, why kill him anyway?" answered Campbell.

"Do you think we can get the CIA to tell us what they know?"

"Maybe, but it would take months, if not years, to do so… unless…" Campbell paused.

"Unless…?" asked Youssef.

"Unless we get the Sunday Times to sort it for us."

Holden's boss, Harold Evans, obliged Campbell and Youssef and the answer came back quickly from the CIA within a few days. There were indeed CIA files on both men but they were classified. The fact that the CIA admitted that they had these files convinced Campbell and Youssef that Holden had connections either to the KGB, or even the CIA itself. So they asked Evans to refer the case to a US court, to force the CIA to release the files to them under the Freedom of Information Act. They flew to Washington together. The sex between them was getting better, intensifying their connection. Campbell was experimenting with her feelings and Youssef was no longer so ridden with guilt about his infidelity to his wife.

They arrived in the US just in time to get to the court: both parties, the Sunday Times and the CIA, had agreed to leave it to the judge to decide whether the files could be released in the public interest. The proceedings took less than five minutes.

A CIA representative was sitting on one side of the court room with two thick files in his hands. The judge asked him to state the reason for the files not being released. "Your Honour, we believe both files contain sensitive information which may jeopardise US national security. You may decide for yourself Your Honour," said the CIA representative, asking permission to approach the bench. The judge signalled for him to come forward and took the two files in his hands. He flicked through the first pages, the entire courtroom held in suspense waiting, wondering. Then the judge slammed the two files shut and gave them back to the CIA rep.

"I hereby rule that the two files shall not be released for public use and shall remain classified due to national security concerns, subject to future reviews." His descending gavel cemented the final verdict. John Bailey, Holden's Sunday Times colleague who had organised the court hearing sat stunned with Campbell and Youssef as the CIA man walked away with the two files. They'd all been certain that the judge would grant them the release of at least Silberman's file, since he had died so many years ago.

The three headed to a nearby bar to take stock of what had just happened. Youssef started the debrief. "Can we assume from what just happened that Holden and or Silberman were involved with the CIA too? Could it be that they were both CIA agents, not KGB agents as we thought?"

"And maybe even liquidated by one of them, or both?" interjected Campbell.

"I can understand why Holden may be relevant to US national security, with his being a journalist, but how can Silberman who died such a long time ago still be relevant?" continued Youssef rhetorically without expecting an answer. But John Bailey shed some light on the decision.

"Guys, do you know who that judge was?" Campbell and Youssef looked puzzled. "That was John Sirica, the judge who sealed the fate of Nixon when he ordered him to handover the Watergate tapes a few years ago. Listen guys, what I mean is that this is not a man who would hesitate to release any material that might implicate anyone if there was any wrongdoing done, so I'm pretty damn sure that the Silberman file contains information that it is still sensitive to this day. But not in the sense of what we are speculating on! Perhaps there were some intercepted messages which may affect important people who are still alive. The best way for you to go forward from here is to go back and find out who exactly that West German fellow, Schmidt, is. In the meantime, if the document that Rivett gave to Silberman in Beirut has any relevance to Holden, that should get us at least somewhere." Campbell and Youssef listened to Bailey's words, and both agreed with him that these might be the only avenues left open. His argument about Sirica's decisive action with Watergate was a strong one.

In the meantime, by pure coincidence, they learnt that Werner Stiller was arriving in the USA to start a new life under a new identity. Campbell requested a supervised meeting with him. During the meeting, Campbell gave Stiller the description of Schmidt that Barron had given them. "This sounds more like Karl-Heinz Schmidt to me, a double agent working for the Stasi. I think he did go to Egypt for two years around that time, helping with East German operations in Africa.

He did this under the cover of being a West German journalist," said Stiller. He then went on to explain how the Soviets were completely wrongfooted when, in 1972, President Sadat expelled them from Egypt; when the Soviets thought Sadat was firmly their man in the region. The KGB took a decision then not to recruit any Egyptians. Later, many other African countries that had aligned themselves with the Soviets also showed signs of breaking away from the Soviet yoke; like Sudan and Somalia to name just two. But Stiller told Campbell and Youssef that he had no idea how Schmidt or the East Germans could be connected to Holden's murder.

29

The thinking surrounding the motive had now shifted for Campbell and Youssef. No longer about Palestine or Egypt, it was about something else. But what? Fortunately, the brigadier was about to have one of his "eureka", or "second car", moments! "Sam," he exclaimed. "Do you remember what the biggest event going on for the Soviets was in 1977, around the time of the murder?" He answered without waiting. "Ogaden! The Ogaden War between Somalia and Ethiopia." He delivered this like a true revelation, an epiphany, with that smile, his smile.

"You might be right! But that means nothing do me and sounds rather niche. Anyway, without a clear motive, where would we even start looking? "

Undeterred by the threat of another long and winding road, they decided to get a proper background on the subject of Ogaden from St. Anthony's College, Oxford where the Yard's outspoken but charming Middle East expert, Elizabeth Monroe, dedicated her academic work to the very regions they needed to know more about. She was more than happy to talk to them. "Many years ago I co-authored a book on Abyssinia, I will help you with anything I remember from this subject, but may I ask first why Scotland Yard and the Egyptian police are both interested in knowing about Ethiopia?"

Campbell explained. "I knew David Holden well actually," mused Monroe. "You know I met him hardly a couple of months before his untimely end. I was incredibly upset… and poor Ruth!"

"Really? When? I mean how? If I may ask…?" said Campbell.

"It was a conference by the Ditchley Foundation, held around October 1977. The conference was about exploring workable solutions between the Israelis and Palestinians, a month before Sadat's peace initiative changed everything. Holden was known for his views on Palestine and was respected by everyone." Monroe even listed for them everyone she remembered attending the conference.

"Did you discuss Africa by any chance?" asked Youssef.

"As a matter of fact we did! Holden did ask me something about Ethiopia, or Somalia rather, during one of the breaks. He asked me a strange question… He asked if I could tell him about the importance of a Somalian document he had."

"And you saw the document?" asked Campbell.

"No, but I recommended he speak to Professor Lewis, the best anthropologist when it comes to Somali history. But, yes, it was strange, in hindsight, he said Lewis was not the right man for the job. Then he said to me 'I know what the document says, but I'm just not sure of its significance.'"

"And then?"

"Nothing, the break was over and that was the last time I spoke to Holden," answered Monroe.

After a pause, Campbell spoke for both investigators: "We think…" she looked at Youssef. "We think that this document might have come to Holden from a gentleman called Leo Silberman. Have you heard of him?"

"Well, now that explains a great deal," answered Monroe. Campbell asked her to elaborate, and she continued. "Of course I've heard of him! … Look, Leo Silberman was an outstanding academic on Africa who put us all to shame, his achievements in such a short life… well… very few academics have managed to do what he did…"

"I sense a 'but' coming! Is there a 'but'?" asked Campbell.

"But," Monroe smiled, "he was a contrarian, obsessed with showing the pitfalls in everyone's argument, rubbed almost everyone up the wrong way. But now I know why Holden said that Professor Lewis was not the right man; Lewis and Silberman never saw eye to eye. You see Silberman didn't have a doctorate to his name, even though he was a professor! But he had many other degrees. I believe that Silberman died while he was doing his PhD on the frontiers of Somalia."

Campbell and Youssef left Oxford convinced that the key to Holden's murder lay in his possession of the document which Rivett had sold to Silberman back in 1960. "It certainly looks this way. If the document has any relevance then it must be that it proves Somalia's right to the Ogaden region. The Soviets would definitely kill to own or suppress that!" said Campbell. "We have to find this document Youssef and we have to know what's in it. Time to go meet with the professor's brother, Freddy Silberman."

*

"I don't want to talk about a family matter to anyone. Leo died 19 years ago… so what if the CIA had a file on him? It doesn't mean anything, and yes he was Holden's lover for many years, they were together until he died in fact, so what?" Freddy Silberman was on the defensive from the start. Neither detective had asked a question yet!

"We're not here about that Mr. Silberman, or about Leo's relationship with Holden. We are here about a different matter," Campbell could do defensive too! And as soon as they told Freddy about Holden having a document related to Somalia he calmed down. Asked them to sit down at last!

"Look, Leo upset many people in his life," he laughed, but the laugh had shades of bitterness. "He would defend communism against Zionists, and Zionism against communists... He enjoyed showing the contradictions in people's logic and naturally no one liked him for that. He started his PhD late in life at UCL. The subject was the Somali-Ethiopian border, but he died without finishing it. He went to Kenya in the summer of 1960, came back in late summer after falling ill and died shortly afterwards. Barely six weeks from the moment he fell ill until he died; it was quick."

"Did Leo mention anything to you about the document? Before he died?" asked Campbell.

"Not directly, but now I remember that he asked me, should anything happen to him, to give a small box full of his papers to David. After he died I looked inside the box, and there was a note at the top presumably intended for Holden, that read, *'If you hear of my death then know that the reason is inside this box'*. I was puzzled by this statement and I showed it to Holden when I gave him the box. He seemed puzzled too... when we looked at the papers they were just academic notes and resources about the Somali-Ethiopian border, nothing struck us as important. So, Holden said that Leo must have meant he died from the stress of doing his PhD, and we both brushed it away as insignificant."

"Was there anything suspicious about Leo's death?" asked Youssef.

"Yes and no. Well, I don't know...maybe. He went to Kenya and Somalia in early summer as I said. He went for a meal with some friends he knew in Nairobi, and the next day he was struck down with what he'd thought was food poisoning, but then it went on and on. In the end he was told by a Nairobi doctor that he may have contracted hepatitis, a liver condition, he was rushed back to London, only to die soon after."

"Mr. Silberman, are you suggesting that Leo's death may have been suspicious?"

"I'm not suggesting anything. Leo himself wondered that before he died, he thought that his symptoms were similar to those experienced by people who ingested a rat poison, 'Klerat' he called it. But he wouldn't tell us why he thought that," answered Freddy.

"And how did Holden receive the news?" asked Campbell.

"He was devastated, they were devoted to each other. Holden organised and wrote the obituary for Leo in The Times a couple of days after; in fact Holden knew more about my brother than all of us! He claimed that Leo had completed a book on the Horn of Africa which was going to be published in the USA, posthumously, but it never was. Everything had been kept in the box I gave him, I'm sure of that. By the way, have you tried the University Library? They should have copies of Leo's papers I'd have thought."

"Do you know who your brother was talking to in Africa before he died?"

"Most of Leo's friends were connected to Africa one way or another, but when he was doing his PhD. he used to speak to Mariano, the legendary Michael Mariano, a leader of the Somali Youth League. Mariano had led Somalia to independence in 1960 and was a hero of Somali irredentism at the time."

"Thank you, Mr. Silberman, for your candid and thoughtful responses," Campbell said as they were leaving. "We'll check at the University Library now…"

After some serious badge flashing at the Senate House Library the next day, the whole bundle of Silberman's papers was in front of them. Many pages of typed up thesis with chapter headings, that they split between them and started reading. Until Campbell saw a cyclostyled copy of a document referred to in the thesis as "obtained by the author through personal contacts".

From: James Hayes Sadler, Colonial Administrator of British Somaliland
To: Musa Arwal of Habir Yunis with 1,793 camels and

382 heads in season living in Bohodil area
Date: 24 November 1899

This promissory undertaking secures the right of Musa Arwal's tribe (Bani Hadder branch) to graze in the winter and, if they so wish, permanently settle in Walwal and its immediate surrounding areas under the protection of this office. Such undertaking is valid for fifty years from the above date. The tribe shall in return promise not to be involved in any trade in slavery, to keep the peace on the road from Bohodil to Walwal and immediately report to the administrator's office any traffic or dealing in slavery by other tribes in the area.

Signed
James Hayes Sadler
(English translation to be kept in Colonial Office, Whitehall, London)

(handwritten note in Amheric)
For proper translation and to include as a footnote Article II of treaty [unclear word] to inform Rodd that if they choose to settle in our land then the Arwal tribe shall be regarded as our subjects.
[Seal of His Majesty the Emperor Menelek II]

This had to be the document Rivett sold to Leo Silberman in the summer of 1960. At face value the document seemed brutally underwhelming, how could anyone be excited about a simple letter like this? More, why would anyone trouble themselves to buy a document about cattle grazing rights, and even pay money for it! They assumed the document must be proof for an argument on the Somali side regarding its claim over Ogaden and that Holden had this original document on him when he died, probably intending to alert the world to its relevance and importance. It fitted well with what Abdul-A'atti told them, that Holden took out a document from his briefcase and showed it to his killers who had to turn on the dome light to read it. Perhaps he'd been hoping they would let him go after they got the document.

So the next port of call for this protracted and convoluted investigation had to be a high-ranking Somali politician; one who might know about the subject. But Campbell and Youssef had started to suspect everyone around them.

30

Many "Palestines" were created by Britain's colonial policy. Entire countries were lost or gained in the realpolitik of London's Foreign Office. But there was nothing else like Ogaden. It was lost by one – or gained by another – in the translation between two languages, literally. Unlike Palestine, the barren region of Ogaden, now part of Ethiopia, had no biblical rights or promissory declarations. Only a plethora of agreements jammed against the rickety wall of history. Like Palestine, its truth is hidden between two wars, not in the clear waters of the fight. Ogaden was in essence a Somali land with its own Somali tribes thriving on it for most of the year until they moved on, nomadically. But all that changed in 1896 at the mountain of Aba Gerima, near the town of Adwa, almost a country away from the sleepy desert of Ogaden.

The battle of Adwa in 1896 had nothing to do with the British, it was between the Ethiopians and Italians, and the latter were defeated, badly. Ethiopians call the battle site Mindibdib, which means "total annihilation", for that's exactly what it was for the Italians. The immediate effect was to halt Europe's colonial scramble for Africa, and to make the presiding Emperor Menelik II legendary.

What happened after that was a story of deceits bound in truths, and truths wrapped in deceits. The Horn of Africa was already divided between three colonial powers, the British, French and Italians. Their interests were in the coastal strips, so Ethiopia was a mere hinterland; the occasional raids by their tribes on coastal towns was only a nuisance. So when Menelik flexed his muscles at the world by crushing the Italians, it all came as a surprise. With the Italians defeated and out of the way, the British and French competed to please the victorious king. Lavish presents were sent him and he made no attempt to hide his pleasure in receiving them, in fact he expected them.

At that time, the British wanted to secure the waters of the Nile for their Egyptian cotton and the French wanted security for their port in Djibouti. And even if Ogaden was a thorny land politically, the British cared very much for its "Haud" area. If Ogaden was the shell, then the Haud was its kernel: a long strip of land with many springs, making it fertile and vital for grazing to the Somali tribes. That was the consensus when Lord Rennel Rodd signed the first Anglo-Ethiopian Agreement in May 1897. Ogaden was just a footnote in that agreement and was effectively "lost" to the Ethiopians, a singular failure of negotiation that haunted Lord Rodd to the day he died, and continued to haunt many who came after him. But later, Britain used every opportunity to backtrack on that agreement, without being seen as a breaker of promises. Even in the early fifties, Ernest Bevin tried, unsuccessfully, to claim Ogaden back from Ethiopia after the Second World War. But that fluke win over Italy by the Ethiopians at Adwa shaped the new borders of Ethiopia. And yet all events in history are born out of the seeds of their previous nuclei.

Before the all-powerful Menelik II became Emperor of Ethiopia, an even more powerful emperor held sway there, Yohannes IV, the King of Kings. He built the foundation of Ethiopia and its walls; Menelik came later and built the roof. Yohannes' vision was that the country, to be strong against Egypt, must have religious uniformity. He wanted to weed out religious allegiances to external powers: the Catholics' allegiance to Rome and the Muslims' allegiance to Istanbul and Cairo. He considered this a source of weakness in a nation, so he rebranded Christianity into a new faith, called Tawahedo, "united in one", which he later made the only authorised religion in Ethiopia. In May 1878, he created a council in which he declared that everyone had to convert to the Tawahedo faith and an ultimatum was issued.

Among those forced to convert was a powerful Muslim imam who was also an able army commander. His name was Mohammed Ali, the ruler of the Wollo Province. Ali was a source of suspicion to many Ethiopian nobility and the Emperor, due to his sympathies with the Ottomans. But convert he did, finally, and he was publicly baptised. His name became Mika'el Ali of Wollo. Yohannes was so pleased with this public relations coup he stood as his godfather and, to cement the bond even further, he invited him to marry one of the nobility, who was coincidentally Menelik's eldest daughter.

This marriage proved very fruitful; in fact Ali was the one who led the Ethiopian army to victory against the Italians in the Battle of Adwa while his father-in-law was emperor. To thank him for the victory that had immortalised his reign, the dying Menelik selected Lij Iyasu, Ali's son, to be his successor. But a power struggle ensued and Iyasu was never actually crowned, though he did rule for three years. A close friend of Iyasu's was a Syrian rubber merchant called Hasib Ydlibi who had had some influence during the reign of Menelik too. But the Ethiopian nobility didn't like the power that Ydlibi had over "their" Iyasu. They suspected he was an Ottoman agent, and so did the British. When Ydlibi became a governor of Harar, the British felt their interests were threatened.

No one knows exactly how the document that Silberman bought ended up in the hands of this Hasib Ydlibi, but that's exactly where it found itself. Upon his death, it passed to his daughter May. She kept it right up until WW2 when it fell in Adrian Harris-Rivett's hands.

Much later, when London became aware of the two contradictory promises Britain had made in the area, it was covered up within the corridors of Whitehall. The document was written in 1899, two years after Lord Rodd's mission. It proved the British government's duplicity, intended or not.

So how did the document get to Adrian Harris-Rivett? It is known that the document stayed in France up to 1929 when it was mysteriously handed to an Ethiopian nobleman chief, Abebe Aregai. Aregai had been a nationalist leader in the struggle against the Italians in the thirties. But when Italy decided to join the axis powers with Germany against Britain and France in June 1940 the game changed and the dynamic of power in the Horn of Africa shifted. After the Dunkirk-style evacuation of British Somaliland in August 1940, the Ethiopians and Somalis felt that the Allied superpowers like Britain and France were both aligned with them against Italy. They had put their animosity aside and both were fighting under the British command of a Somali army "company", and the commander was Captain Adrian Harris-Rivett.

Aged only 32 at that time, he'd made the rank of captain relatively young, but rose to the challenge the war created with a wisdom and integrity beyond his years. As the British were hopelessly outnumbered, he led his Somali troops through the most difficult of situations into safety; an "honourable retreat" as it was called then. It was summer, in searing heat, in one of the most inhospitable areas of the world and they were 70 miles from the nearest British troops.

Under his command at this point, Harris-Rivett had a small contingent of around 500 Ethiopian fighters, led by chief Aregai, who were fighting alongside the Somalis for the British. He knew how the Somalis and Ethiopians felt about each other, even though they were fighting a common enemy, so he had kept them apart. But simple maths was against the company and the honourable retreat was ordered from the central command. Harris-Rivett took the whole company to the port at Berbera ready for evacuation to Aden.

On arriving in Berbera, another order from central command came: to leave the Ethiopian troops behind. Again. Harris-Rivett left the armed Ethiopians at a place called Shiikh thinking they would be able to fight the Italians should they get that far. But as Harris-Rivett was embarking on a ship at Berbera, destined to take them to Adan, it came to his attention that the Ethiopians had later been stripped of the weapons he'd left them by another British Army commander. That infuriated Harris-Rivett and he heroically decided to leave his ship, return with a few loyal troops, cutting right through the advancing Italians, to get the weapons back to the abandoned Ethiopian soldiers. It was only then that the Ethiopian chief Aregai gave Harris-Rivett the document, asking him to keep it safe due to its importance. It was also a gesture of solidarity from a grateful Ethiopian to the Somali people, made out of gratitude to them. He hoped the Civil Service in London would take seriously the injustice done to Somalis with regard to the Ogaden.

Harris-Rivett was later decorated with a medal for his initiative and bravery in saving his troops in Somaliland. But he hadn't given the piece of paper he acquired for safe keeping, still wrapped in an old cloth, a second thought. Even in 1960, when he sold the document to Leo Silberman in Lebanon, he didn't appreciate its full significance. He never understood its significance; only Leo Silberman did.

31

For someone who in 1977 had only been abroad once, Sam Campbell was now really notching up the airmiles. Freddy Silberman's lead, Michael Mariano, was a Somali diplomat based in their embassy in Zambia but he agreed to meet the detectives in Cairo. Could this be the closing stage that would reveal the truth about Holden's murder?

"How can I help you both? You said you have something to show me?" said Mariano, as though it was all so reassuringly simple! After listening to the two detectives, he offered them a brief summary of Somalia's complex colonial past and uncertain future.

"It seems that Britain has a habit of entering into too many contradictory agreements, promising different peoples different things," said Youssef when Mariano finished.

"Yep, exactly so. Another unholy mess created by the British, just like with Palestine. The Anglo-Ethiopia Treaty was signed in 1897, such a long time before 1954 when it was finally ratified by Britain, thereby sealing the fate of Ogaden and handing the area back to Ethiopa: it was myopic in the extreme. Those who lived in the Ogaden area were always Somali. Back in 1955, I led a delegation to the UN arguing that the 1897 agreement was null and void, illegal. But we didn't have enough evidence to prove our claim."

"And that's where Silberman comes in?" guessed Campbell.

"Exactly! Leo was secretly helping us, that's why he did his PhD. on the frontiers of Somalia, but we couldn't prove anything, until…" Mariano lowered his voice. "One day he sent me a letter, early summer 1960, it said that he had found an original document that may prove the illegality of the 1897 Anglo-Ethiopia Treaty hence the illegality of its subsequent ratification. So we agreed to meet in Mogadishu. Travel wasn't easy or cheap in those days, but he said he needed to meet someone in Lebanon first, and then go on to Nairobi before we met. We didn't hear anything more from him after he went to Kenya. He never made it to Mogadishu."

"Hmmmm, yes…" said Campbell.

Youssef took up the slack. " Any conversations about the document since then?"

"After Leo died we forgot about it altogether, we didn't know what was in the document anyway until 1977, in the build-up to the Ogaden War. Our President, Siad Barre, tasked me to chair a committee to prove the legality of Somalia's claim over Ogaden. Barre needed to argue the legality of his case. So that was when I remembered Silberman's document and I did mention its existence to Barre. I had no way of finding out what happened to it."

"Did he ask you to find it?" asked Youssef.

"Sort of, later. Barre was playing a dangerous game in 1977, when he asserted Somali sovereignty over Ogaden. It all got a bit communist! In February of that year the Soviets floated the idea of creating a socialist federation of states in the Horn of Africa, with Ethiopia, Somalia and South Yemen all orbiting in the Soviet sphere of influence. The next month, the Cuban leader Fidel Castro called for a summit meeting of these states in Aden. The discussions about Ogaden got heated. Barre challenged Castro that if the federation was "socialist" then the people of Ogaden should be able to choose whether to be part of Somalia or Ethiopia, but Castro didn't like this and cited 'internationally recognised borders'."

"And Barre mentioned that document to him?"

"Worse. It was not diplomacy's finest hour! President Barre accused Castro of perpetuating an imperialist British mess, adding he had damning proof that the British acted illegally when the "internationally recognised borders" were agreed in 1897. Castro was furious, he felt insulted by Barre. He made it clear that Barre had overstepped his mark."

"And then?" asked Youssef.

"And then Barre took the decision to invade the Ogaden region in July 1977, which was very bad timing."

"Why so?"

"There was no way we were ready. Okay, maybe we were ready to fight the Ethiopians... but not fight the Cubans! Even more stupidly..." Mariano looked like he wanted to backtrack but lowered his voice instead, closing his eyes momentarily. "Yes! *Stupidly,* Barre tried to obtain arms from both the Soviets and America after this invasion. The Soviets were not impressed with him, since Ethiopia was firmly in the Soviet sphere of influence. To cut a long story short, when Barre later visited Saudi Arabia in August, I was in his delegation. David Holden was writing a book on Saudi Arabia then, and we both met. He told me that he had found Silberman's evidence. So I kept in touch with him during the months following until we agreed to meet in Cairo in December."

"And did the meeting take place?" asked Youssef.

"Of course it didn't. Holden was killed, just like Silberman…"

At that point Campbell thought it only right to show Mariano a copy of the document. Mariano read it in a kind of awe. It might have been the Holy Grail to him.

"Do you have the original?"

"No, but we think Holden's killers now do," answered Campbell.

"This, my dear lady, is the proof that the 1897 and 1954 agreements which Britain signed with Ethiopia were illegal and should be nullified in an international court of law. If we'd had the original document back then, the Ogaden would have been part of Somalia by now. There's no doubt that superpowers would kill over a document like this. And I happen to know that Silberman was going to publish this document in a quarterly journal, "Confluence" I believe it was called, using his American contact."

"Do you know who the contact was?" asked Campbell.

"Yes, someone close to Henry Kissinger who edited this journal. America was trying to exert pressure on Britain at that time, just like they did with the Suez Crisis. But the document was never published as we know. In fact it never made it into American hands."

It seemed the case of the murdered English journalist was finally solved. But neither Youssef nor Campbell quite felt the euphoria of closure, which was strange given the years the case had been haunting them. Nevertheless, the closure certainly seemed real and as they prepared to go their separate ways, Youssef in a car back to his wife and one point five children, she on a plane back to… whatever her life was, they both agreed that the affair between them had to end. In farewell, at the airport Youssef gave her a bouquet of flowers. She was deeply touched by that, and even saw it as an effort to "do the English thing" just for her. Though in truth giving flowers had been an Egyptian tradition for over a thousand years. And with flowers, love, sex compartmentalised again, for good this time, Youssef used their last moments together to ask Campbell if she thought Scotland Yard would pursue the investigation in a court of law, or even take it up with the Soviets.

"I still don't think we can prove anything, Youssef. Even here in Egypt you can't prove anything. Of course, you could get Abdul-A'atti based on his confession, but do you think Egypt will benefit from showing the world an Egyptian police officer was involved in the murder of a famous British journalist? Even the British wouldn't want you to do that, since Abdul-A'atti would point his fingers at Barron in London and the whole world would think it was the British who were behind Holden's murder after all. Think about it!"

"But Barron may confess too and point to the real killers, the Stasi."

"If he did confess, and I doubt he would testify in court, can you imagine the nuisance it would cause to the global détente that we are witnessing between the Western world and the Communist Bloc? No, the Yard will want to keep the secrets of Holden's murder just that, secrets, buried forever," said Campbell as she felt her lover's gentle hand on hers.

"I have never before worked on a case that no one wants solved," said Youssef with a tinge of sadness and resignation. Campbell nodded her head as she disappeared among the crowd of Cairo departures.

*

On arriving to the reality of London, Campbell got word that Maurice Oldfield wanted to meet her again, same café, and as it happened the same table too. But had he anticipated her anger? Probably…

"Did MI6 have anything to do with Silberman's death?"

"I asked you to stick within the scope of your investigation, which was Holden, but you had to dig deeper didn't you?" answered Oldfield.

"Maybe, just maybe," began Campbell through gritted teeth, "that's because no one can solve a murder without knowing the motive!"

"Listen to me Campbell! Silberman meddled in something which was beyond his academic interests, the timing of that document he bought couldn't have been worse for Britain… we'd only just extricated ourselves from the Mau Mau uprising in Kenya…"

"And so he was eliminated. And Holden had to pay the same price…" Campbell looked disgusted. There was something about Oldfield that made her exaggerate her reactions. Perhaps subconsciously she was flirting with his past observation that she was "wonderfully feisty"!

"This is what we wanted you to find out for us, and you did. You uncovered that the Soviets were behind Holden's murder. Kim Philby played us, twice," said Oldfield.

"What? Philby witnessed Rivett selling the old document to Silberman, I know that much…" conceded Campbell. She thought of Barron's paratrooper strategy, the "need to know" allocation of information and resources. What she wanted from Oldfield was the whole picture, no matter how big it was.

Maybe the experienced man from Six knew he'd exhausted her patience. And maybe he respected her too much to let that stand. He opened up. "It was Philby who tipped us off about Silberman's having a document that would damage British interests back in 1960. But after he switched, and defected to the Soviet Union, it was the same Philby who tipped off the KGB in 1977 about Holden having ownership of the same document that would damage Soviet interests in the Horn of Africa."

"I can understand why Philby would tip off the KGB about Holden in 1977, he was their spy after all, living in Moscow, but tipping us off in 1960 about Silberman… why?" asked Campbell.

"In 1960 Philby was out alone in the wilderness of Beirut. He was keen to ingratiate himself back into Six while still keeping in contact with the KGB, so to prove himself to us, he fed us a few tips about various Soviet activities, some innocuous stuff that wouldn't rile the Russians, and while doing so he tipped us off about Silberman's latest purchase…"

"So it was the uninvited guest all along!"

Oldfield wasn't sure of the reference, but he wasn't a man to waste time on unimportant threads. "Quite right. Little did the KGB know that 17 years later that document would become their number one problem too! And the swine gave the KGB his blessing to eliminate Holden, even though they'd been friends since way back."

It came as a relief to Campbell; not just the overdue outing of the perpetrator, straight from the horse's mouth so to speak, but the fact that someone else seemed angry! *Appropriately, given his nickname,* Campbell reflected, *this dénouement seems fresh out of a le Carré novel.* But Smiley wasn't finished.

"Did you know the traitor also had a *personal* interest in Holden's case?"

"How do you mean?" asked Campbell.

Oldfield placed his brown hat on his head – a precursor to bidding her and their coffee shop table, an adieu.

"As I told you before DCI, not everything is quite what it seems." He left some change for his own cup of tea on the table. "I wish you a happy life, Campbell. Well done by the way!" and he disappeared.

32

Snell asked Campbell to write a report of her findings, to include everything whether important or not. This was standard procedure to close down the investigation, to put it to bed as a "murder connected with international espionage", outside Scotland Yard's remit. She dreaded the task. The idea was almost as brutal as the murder itself. But she did write her report, correcting her old versions of it time and time again. Every statement needed corroborating; cross referencing was needed for every interview. *Pointless,* Campbell thought to herself, *unless the Soviets own up to it, no one will find the real murderers.*

The next day she tidied up her report, added exhibits and appendices, ready to submit it to Snell. Hopefully for good. In the morning, sitting, waiting, restless outside Snell's office, she turned from the tall office window that looked out onto the back quadrangle, and decided to give her report a last casual check. Her eyes fell on a page printed off Werner Stiller's microfiche. She was not sure she'd read this document before. Karston Koenig had sent it over a few months after their meeting – but she'd ignored it, deeming that angle finished. The document wasn't even translated into English. But she might as well try to resurrect her school German while she waited. The parts she understood made her freeze.

Document A.X.COR.892351

Minutes of Meeting
Date: 23 May 1977
Venue: HVA Headquarter - Berlin

Present in meeting:

1. Comrade x - Soviet KGB
2. Comrade y - Democratic Germany HVA Stasi
3. Comrade z - Cuban foreign intelligence services

Item 12 - Potential Conflict in the Horn of Africa - Ganymede

The matter raised by Comrade z in last month's meeting was discussed again.

Comrade x: We asked Sonny if he knew anything about this English journalist. He told us that he'd known him well during his time in Beirut and that he guesses the document Siad Barre may be referring to is the same one he saw being sold to his old lover professor. Apparently Sonny's father saw the document and told Sonny of its content at the time. Therefore my instruction, comrades, is to eliminate any possibility of this document seeing the light of day. We would like to ask you to take care of this operation.
Comrade y: Our contacts seem to be indicating that the Mossad are planning to eliminate him but aren't sure how yet, I mean we do not know their plans at this stage.
Comrade z: But we do, comrade, they are trying to trick the Egyptians into doing it on their behalf, unwittingly.
Comrade x: How can this be possible? They are arch enemies, are you sure about your sources?
Comrade z: Yes, comrade. They plan to trick them into thinking that he is another English journalist, one the Egyptians already identified as a target for their own reasons.
Comrade x: Very clever! The Mossad never cease to amaze!

Comrade y: But hang on comrades, think about it, why don't we tag along with them? I mean do the same thing as them, make them think they are doing it but this time for us too.

Some discussion took place on the practicality of Comrade y's proposal and the risks involved and it was concluded,

Comrade x: Go ahead but we shall leave it to you comrades to work out the details, see any blind spots and synergies for you to piggyback onto the Mossad's operation. That should please Sonny no end!

Item concluded for this meeting and considered closed.

"You may come in now, DCI Campbell, he's ready to see you," said Snell's secretary, but Campbell could not move. The murder wasn't solved fully as she thought. She still had more loose ends to tie, or rather tied ends to unravel. Campbell looked at the secretary, dazed, confused, then turned and walked away. Leaving her report on the chair and slowly leaving the building, she faded into the bustling London crowds.

33

Blown by the wind of peace across Decapolis.
On the way from Damascus to Philadelphia,
Urged by a certain call of nature,
The ruins of Gerasa, a man chooses.
"Is this how my citadels are used?" asks the Emperor.
"In peace a citadel makes a fine stopover."

Dave H
December 1st, 1977

So read the writing on the back of the postcard. On the front was a photo of the citadel of Jerash in Jordan. It was a beautiful August day in 1980 when Campbell received it, anonymously, inside an envelope that had been posted from Jordan. The card was unfranked and addressed to Jan Morris at the Sunday Times in London.

Campbell checked her files. Holden was on his way from Damascus to Amman with Edward Mortimer and Wilbur G. Landry on that date. She didn't show the card to anyone but asked Mortimer to confirm. He said yes, he vaguely remembered that they did stop over in the city of Jerash and had a break there. And naturally they'd answered calls of nature there too! They'd spent around one hour resting and looking around. Though Mortimer didn't see Holden writing a postcard, he did remember Holden asking if there was a post office nearby before they left Jerash. Clearly this card was a predecessor to the one Morris received close to Christmas. The one that bore a continuation of the same poem:

> Pray for the peace of Jerusalem.
> Citadels still have their uses.

That couplet now made perfect, albeit jocular and trivial, sense. Ah, the importance of context! Holden was telling Morris that he'd taken a detour to Jerusalem after all, and that he'd used the citadel in the same way he had in Jerash. At a time of peace, old ruins of citadels make good urinals.

Why had Holden thought that he had already sent the first card to Morris when he clearly hadn't, and why was she receiving it now? Campbell could only think that Holden must have asked someone, perhaps someone employed at the Intercontinental Hotel in Amman, to send the card for him. A person who had probably forgotten or misplaced the card and was now sending it on in case it helped. Maybe someone like Adnan the bellboy.

34

The Jordanian Airline flight attendant, Nicki Webster, hadn't noticed the note which Holden surreptitiously placed in her waistcoat pocket – not until she was in Washington, two days after flight RJ503 had landed in Cairo.

She just thought it was a prank. There was nothing about Holden in the news at that time – Holden's body hadn't been identified then – so it sat as a screwed-up paper ball in her hotel room's waste bin before being subsumed into the general Washington trash the next morning. It wasn't until Webster arrived in Heathrow, on her way back to Jordan, that she saw a newspaper headline about a journalist named David Holden having been shot dead in Cairo. The thing was, she no longer remembered what the note had said, let alone the name or the number of the man it had asked her to contact.

She did recall that the Sunday Times was mentioned, so she gave them a call:

"Sunday Times, can I help you?"

"I'd like to speak to the editor."

"May I ask what it is regarding?"

"Information relating to the killing of David Holden."

After some pause, "May I ask your name please?"

"Nicki Webster. I was the air hostess who served Mr. Holden on his way from Amman to Egypt."

The operator put her through, but there was a much longer pause this time. Webster was close to hanging up. "Hello, Miss Webster," a voice spoke just in time. "You have information on David Holden? I was his colleague. The editor is out right now, but you can talk to me."

"Thanks. I was the member of cabin crew who served him. I remember him a little, I think. But I'm ringing you because he slipped a note into my uniform pocket which may be connected to his death."

"I see. Do you have the note with you? What did it say?"

"I don't have it any more I'm afraid, but it said something like he'd been approached during the flight by a man who wanted him to interview someone … there was a name and number in it but I'm afraid I threw the note away. I thought it was a prank."

"Right, okay. Did you tell anyone else about this?"

"No, you're the first person I've spoken to about it."

"Good! Don't tell anyone else just yet. We'll get the police to contact you. Thank you, Miss Webster. You did the best you could."

Later Webster took a shower; she had to leave her Heathrow hotel for the flight to Jordan. Exiting the ensuite she saw a man, Middle Eastern in appearance, sitting on her bed. She tried to scream but another man appeared and placed his hand over her mouth.

"We are not here to harm you, Nicki, we came to give you a message but first we need you to keep quiet." It was the man sitting down who spoke, without any discernible accent. Webster, scared, nodded her head to show her compliance and the second man stood back.

"Forget about the note from Holden. Wipe it from your memory, for Tom's sake." Tom, Nicki's six-year-old son, and was being looked after by her mother at home in Middlesbrough. Nicki promised to comply with their wish and the two men left her alone.

Shaking, sobbing, Nicki Webster made another phone call after the two men had left. "Mum? It's me. I'm coming home."

"LOOSE ENDS"

DCI Sam Campbell: retired early from Scotland Yard after representing the UK in an investigation into a South American religious massacre. Her role helped to oust the ruling military dictatorship in the country involved. After the reunification of Germany, even in retirement, Campbell made several visits to the Stasi archive to look for more documents on Holden but did not even find the documents which Werner Stiller brought with him let alone any new relevant material. She was later diagnosed with cancer of the pancreas and died in 1996 aged 63, childless and a recluse. The following words are inscribed on her gravestone, *"You should not honour men (or women) more than the truth"*. No one in her family knows why she chose those words or what they meant.

Colonel Nabil Hassan Ali Youssef: was pensioned off from the Egyptian police force after the public assassination of President Sadat in October 1981. He never recovered from the shock of the "disgrace" of his early retirement. Later he became a small businessman but died in 2002 and was buried in Cairo. He refused to talk about the Holden murder until his death but continued to claim that the investigation had made him many powerful enemies in the government. He never met with Sam Campbell again and never talked to anyone about her, but he'd secretly kept a photograph taken of them together in Washington DC. It was hidden inside one of his books and was discovered by chance, by a street bookseller, many years later.

Major Ahmed Mukhtar Faisal: later promoted under the reign of President Mubarak in Egypt to become Head of the Criminal Investigation Department. Still alive but now old and retired, he claims to have little recollection of the Holden murder and downplays his involvement in it.

Captain Sayyed Hassan Mahmoud: retired from the Egyptian police force in 2006 with a relatively low rank. Nothing is known about him after that.

Eileen Gibson: took Cyprus as her permanent home and continued writing as a freelance journalist for various publications on Middle Eastern affairs, later focusing on Islamic cultural history. She died in 1999 in Cyprus in a nursing home, alone.

Nicki Webster: Six years after her call to the Sunday Times newspaper, she was diagnosed with severe Paranoid Personality Disorder… maybe because she'd been caught in the fallout from the international murder of David Holden.

www.ingramcontent.com/pod-product-compliance
Lightning Source LLC
Chambersburg PA
CBHW030257100526
44590CB00012B/429